Pleiadian Master Teachings

Concepts From the Realms of Light

Michael Love

Sacred Light Publishing

Contents

Dedication

This book is dedicated first to my loving wife, Lara, who is my primary inspiration for bringing this information to the world. She saw the light within me even when I did not see it and encouraged me to keep going against all odds. She is my best friend and the most wonderful partner. Thank you for standing beside me through it all, and may this book be the highest blessing for you. Secondly, this work is dedicated to all the Starseeds of planet Earth. The great ones who came to Earth with great purpose and intention to create a better world here for all. Thank you for everything you have done and for your dedication to humanity.

The highest blessings,
Michael Love

Foreword

Down through the ages, the Pleiadians have been guiding the evolution of humanity by bringing higher knowledge to planet Earth.

These grand beings are master teachers of advanced spirituality and metaphysics, and their teachings are encoded in a special way to trigger dormant DNA strands and expand consciousness levels.

The Pleiadians teach that light is information and darkness is the lack of information. This book is filled with pure light, and as one takes this light in, their eyes will open to many new possibilities and realities.

The Pleiadians know that a solid foundational understanding of universal concepts is first required to achieve spiritual and scientific mastery. The Pleiadian Master Teachings book describes how the universe works in an easy-to-understand way and is also the perfect operator's manual for living life to the fullest.

This book contains many profound and eye-opening insights that serve as practical guidance for ultimate self-realization.

Let's begin with the foundation of the universe and work our way to planet Earth.

Chapter 1: Consciousness

"The ultimate knowledge one can attain is to become fully aware of who and what they truly are."
The Pleiadians

It is one thing to go deep into meditation and eventually come face to face with the highest being in the universe; however, it is a much more profound thing to find out the identity of that being.

I remember the defining moment on my ascension journey years ago before I began channeling the Pleiadians when I truly woke up, and everything changed dramatically. I had experienced a profound NDE from an auto crash where I found myself 50 feet up in the air, looking down at my deceased body lying on the highway. I recall so clearly asking myself at that moment. "If my body is down on the ground and I am up here looking at it, what am I? Some answer this question truthfully by saying one's ultimate essence is spirit or soul; however, after contemplating a bit deeper during this incredible experience, I came to the following conclusions.

I first determined that I was the one who was watching, so I said, "I am the watcher."

I then proclaimed. "I am the observer."

After much deeper reflection, while hovering in this out-of-body state, I further proclaimed, "I am the one who is aware."

Then the ultimate realization came to me, producing this universal sense of awe.

I said, "I know what I am. I am consciousness."

I said, "This is my identity."

At that point, I knew 'what I was,' and the notion of it was staggering, but I had not yet pondered on the 'who I was' part.

Further into my NDE, I began traveling through the tunnel of light, and the light I was moving toward appeared to be a blinding white sun. It did not look like a god or a human, but as I moved closer to this gigantic ball of white light, I could sense that whatever was behind it was alive, very intelligent, and was indeed what is called God. The tunnel I was moving through was also not just a tunnel but a portal or wormhole, and I wasn't walking through it; I was flying through it at the speed of light. The space I was traveling through passed by as colorful flashes of light. It was the galaxy's vastness, and I was headed directly for this massive white light.

When I emerged from the other end of this galactic travel way, close to this giant white sun, I landed on what seemed like a platform. This landing platform was situated amid a beautiful celestial and natural paradise. I noticed the giant white sun was shining in the background skies and was the light for this incredible celestial world. The buildings and structures in this world were made of pastel-colored, transparent crystal; there were millions of more colors in this realm, everything was in high-definition, and nature abounded.

As soon as I arrived in this divine world, I found myself standing before twelve of the most beautiful beings I had ever encountered. They looked very human and did not have wings on their backs. There were males and females, and their bodies were more transparent than Earth bodies. They emitted a pure love that I had never felt back on Earth. These celestial beings did not speak with words but by telepathy. When they communicated, they said, Michael, "We are the angels of your bible." "We are also the extra-terrestrials many have seen in Earth's skies." "We are your family, and you are one of us."

They said, "We are the Pleiadians, and you are in the fifth dimension."

After telling me these things, they said, "You must go back to Earth now. You are doing something important there, and you must return and finish this work."

Pleiadians are known for being rebels, and after I thought about their suggestion, I said, "Life on Earth can be full of pain and suffering, and sometimes it can be unpleasant to be there. Therefore, I do not wish to go back there only to experience more pain, so I choose to stay with you in this beautiful paradise."

These magnificent beings said, "You have free will, so you may do anything you desire." They said, "We can see the bigger picture and want what is best for you. So we are guiding you to return to Earth because what you are working on there will help many people."

I did not see the importance of this divine guidance at that moment, so being stubborn and trying to avoid any further pain on Earth, I insisted on staying right where I was, in paradise! After much time passed, what seemed like eons, and after further counsel about returning to Earth, I proposed a deal to these magnificent beings of light. I told them, "If you show me who is behind that massive white sun, then I will return to Earth." It was indeed a grand request because I was asking to find out the identity of God, the very creator of the universe. The Pleiadian beings I communicated with began smiling and laughing about my bold request. Finally, one of these beings, a female Pleiadian, came close and said, "Very well, we will show you the identity of the one behind the light."

The grand Pleiadians proceeded to dim the light of this blinding white sun, and as I looked, I saw a human-looking figure start to appear out of the white light. It was walking directly toward me. In a moment, I was standing face-to-face with it so close that our noses were almost touching, and we were staring directly into each other's eyes.

What I saw was so shocking that it shook my soul. I only saw myself, and in that super-intense moment, I remember asking, how can this be?

Likewise, when you come face-to-face with the highest being in the cosmos, you will inevitably discover that it was you all along. This higher truth cannot be conceived from a third-dimensional point of view. Still, as one's consciousness expands, one will be given this ultimate truth.

"No being in the vastness of the universe is higher or greater than you."
The Pleiadians

We will discuss this great being more in Chapter 11 on sovereignty. This greatness is who and what you truly are in all your glory. Maybe it will take some time to know this fully, but the fact of who and what you are remains the same.

You are the light, you are consciousness, and you are no less than God. You are not part of God or even a child of God; you are the entirety of it all. You are all that is. You are this, she is this, he is this, and so are they. Everyone and everything is this. Everyone and everything are the infinite creator, God-conscious energy in expression, manifested as all that is. This is your identity.

One cannot exercise ego and say they are God without saying others are God. God is singular because this is all that exists, and there is nothing that is not this. A simple way of saying this is that

God expresses itself as you. You are God manifested as you.

Knowing who and what you are is one thing, but being this is another. As you become more and more familiar with yourself, your grand unlimited attributes and abilities will become more apparent, and you will begin to exercise them. Eventually, you will be who you truly are in all ways. The Pleiadians love to use humor in their teachings because humor is also a part of God. They like to say, *"You are God, so start acting like it."*

The primary point here is that Consciousness is God, and this is your identity.

There is an infinite, living, organic conscious intelligence which is omnipresent and omnipotent that permeates everything in this universe. It is pure sublime conscious intelligence, the foundational cause behind the universe.

Consciousness is fundamental in all science and spirituality, and nothing can be considered without considering consciousness first. This universal consciousness is an eternal living, loving, life-bearing presence. Its advanced intelligence is displayed throughout creation in mind-boggling ways for all to behold. It manifests its character as pure unconditional love and is the unseen essence of life throughout the universe. Consciousness is uncreated, and it cannot be destroyed. It just is. It always was, and it will always be.

Consciousness is an infinite energy field that creates the conditions to manifest different realities according to sensory perceptions. In this sense, consciousness is a pre-existing, universal presence and fundamental element of mind and matter.

The great creative force of the universe uses universal laws, math, and patterns to build and operate its creations. It constructs and runs advanced universal programs that affect all of creation. It's in the business of connecting everything in the universe. One primary mathematical system it uses, from the macro down to the micro, is The Universal Base Twelve Energy System.

This Universal Base Twelve System is the mathematical foundation of all Pleiadian technology and spirituality.

You will notice how every topic in this writing fits together and synchronizes with this Universal Base System of Twelve.

Consciousness has organized the universe into the following interrelated systems of twelve:

- Twelve States or Levels of Consciousness
- Twelve Dimensions of Frequency
- Twelve Primary Strands of DNA
- Twelve Chakra Energy Centers

Each Base Twelve System is entangled at the quantum level and directly corresponds vibrationally with the other systems.

There are twelve primary states or levels of consciousness in this universe, and each level resonates in different frequency ranges. Each higher level resonates faster than the level below it, and the faster the vibration, the more advanced information it contains.

State	Frequency Range	Qualities	Dimension
Mapped States			
Delta	1-4 Hertz	Rem Sleep	1
Theta	4-8 Hertz	Light Sleep	2
Alpha	7.4-12 Hertz	Twilight State	3
Beta	13-30 Hertz	Alert State	4
Gamma	40-111 Hertz	Bliss State	5
Lambda	100-150 Hertz	Heightened Conscious	6
Epsilon	150-200 Hertz	Super Conscious	7
UnMapped States			
Zeta	200-240 Hertz	Subconscious 1	8
Eta	240-360 Hertz	Subconscious 2	9
Iota	360-420 Hertz	Subconscious 3	10
Kappa	420-600 Hertz	Subconscious 4	11
Mu	666-Unlimited Hertz	God Consciousness	12

The first seven levels shown in the chart above have been discovered and are understood by Earth scientists, but the last five levels on the list are yet to be discovered or accessed by most Earth humans.

Supernatural abilities only begin to operate at the gamma consciousness level and are fully functional in the lambda state of being. We will teach you in Chapter 10 how to achieve these super-conscious states. God-like abilities become more expansive as one moves into the faster states of being at the high end of this universe, from Zeta to Mu Level Consciousness. The Epsilon state on Earth is rare and exists mostly among advanced meditators and certain Buddhist monks. In this state of consciousness, there is no heartbeat, pulse, or breath, yet a being exists, very alive in a state of completely suspended animation. This state slows the speed of reality frames in relation to the consciousness perceiving them. In ancient martial arts, this slowing down of reality gives the warrior plenty of time to see and counter his opponent's every move.

The psychophysiological principle states:
Any experience that one has, one has only while having a specific state of consciousness or brain wave pattern. If their brain wave patterns change, then their experience will change.

When consciousness levels change, the experience perceived by the physical senses also changes. The higher the level of consciousness, the greater the level of sensory perception. What cannot be detected by the senses at lower levels of consciousness becomes easily perceivable at higher levels. Therefore empathic beings have a heightened intuition, feeling everything with super sensitivity and intensity. It's also why high-vibrational beings possess enhanced psychic abilities such as the four clairs, clairaudience (hearing voices), clairvoyance (seeing images), clairsentience (recognizing feelings), and claircognizance (knowing).

When one's consciousness operates at very low frequencies, one is said to be unconscious. One can be awake and functioning at this level but operate mostly unconsciously. In this state, one operates at minimum levels and will only be aware of basic survival needs. All low-vibrational behavioral issues exist in the unconscious state. Unconsciousness is also the vibrational level where so-called accidents, mishaps, and injuries occur.

The beings of planet Earth are currently working to reach the fifth level, or gamma state of consciousness, on their evolutionary journey. We will focus on this state of being here. The fifth-dimensional state of consciousness is called gamma and is experienced as a state of perfection and bliss. The ancient books of Earth referred to this state of being as heaven, nirvana, samadhi, and Shamballa. It is a state of only peace, love, health, abundance, joy, and complete freedom. When one reaches this state and can sustain it, one transcends and overcomes all lower things. Though the gamma state is only level five out of the twelve universal levels of consciousness, great power is found within this state of being.

When the DNA of one's cells begins to resonate at the 40-hertz gamma level, one gains access to heightened gamma consciousness which opens the door to the universe. In this state, one resides above the frequency of neuronal firing and blends with the energy field of the universe. This state of oneness is above all ego and the self. This attainment is the samadhi of yoga and the Nibbana of the Buddha. It is the Brahman and the divine essence of the master Jesus. The most proficient meditators achieve this state and know firsthand that gamma is the pure consciousness energy that manifests itself as the majestic and miraculous characteristics of divinity. Proficient mystics, mediums, and healers naturally resonate in this state of consciousness. They know this high vibrational source energy is a pure stream of consciousness that can heal one's deepest pain and suffering. It not only heals but also heals at once and in a miraculous way. This is just its divine nature.

The gamma level of consciousness has been called 'The power of the angels' as it creates an energetic field that repels all lower vibrational energy fields. This force field of consciousness provides literal divine protection and attracts only divine benevolent guidance.

Everything flows perfectly in the gamma state of consciousness. When one attains it, it is often referred to as being 'in the zone.' Resistance is significantly reduced in this zone, and things become effortless and efficiently work out without issue.

Gamma consciousness produces heightened feelings of love and a connection to all things. It's the feeling you have when you listen to a certain song and is the vibe of being deeply in love. The gamma state is the amazing feeling you have when something awesome happens. It is the most sought-after thing in the universe; whatever the best feeling is, one ever experienced, that is gamma. Gamma is the state of super consciousness, the pure god state of being that any ascended master has attained, where there are no limits to one's abilities. To maintain the gamma state is to reach the guru state and live peacefully, spiritually, and powerfully.

Gamma-level consciousness allows for much higher levels of mental creativity. This is because the right and left brains are synchronized in the gamma state into full harmonic resonance. Master musicians, writers, and artists that operate from this level produce masterpieces. In gamma, one has laser-sharp focus and concentration and achieves high levels of cognitive functioning. Those who maintain a gamma state of being have higher IQs, more mental processing power and speed, and excellent memory recall. In addition, gamma consciousness produces high levels of success among achievers and gives extraordinary physical abilities to top athletes.

The gamma state is also referred to as 'The place of miracles' by spiritual masters because, unlike the lower states of beings where not many nice things happen, incredible miracles come out of nowhere constantly for the being who resonates in this frequency range. One could say God is blessing them much more at this level, and it would be true. It's just that one has elevated their consciousness to be more aligned vibrationally with universal source energy and the unlimited abundance of all that is. At this level, one can manifest their dreams and desires with much more power, speed, and much less effort. It's easy to see why the ancients called this state of being the abode of the gods, nirvana, and bliss.

This fifth level of consciousness is a worthy goal for all the beings of Earth who have labored hard for so long to evolve their consciousness. Therefore, it is a blessing to finally come to a place where one can rest from their labors and all lower sufferings. Furthermore, it is most pleasant to begin receiving and enjoying nicer things as the universe opens and pours out its infinite abundance. These blessings and more will be received by the one who does the necessary work to elevate their level of being.

The fifth level of consciousness is only the beginning of heaven, and as one's consciousness keeps expanding, one will walk into the heavens that exist above the heavens.

Planet Earth is rapidly moving into the golden new age of light, where the gamma state of consciousness will be the norm. As the great awakening of humanity moves into high gear, and as more and more light shines in this world, heaven on Earth will soon be realized. When the beings of Earth reach this higher level of gamma consciousness, this entire realm will instantly be transformed into the paradise it was always meant to be.

Chapter 2: Vibration

"Always vibrate high!"
The Pleiadians

In Chapter 1, we established that consciousness is the foundational energy source of the universe. Then, we discussed the twelve states of consciousness divided into vibrational frequency ranges.

In quantum physics, this vibrating field of universal conscious energy is called the quantum field or the field of unlimited possibilities of existence. These unlimited possibilities are vibrating waves of energy from which all things in the universe manifest. Even matter at its smallest level is composed of these vibrating energy waves. The scientific formula $E=MC2$ backs this up accurately and says that everything in the universe is energy. This energy that makes up all things is in an eternal state of vibration.

Knowledge about the universal law of vibration and the idea of "vibes" has existed for a long time. The hermetic doctrine handed down from ancient Atlantis best describes the universal law of vibration. It says, "Nothing rests; everything moves; everything vibrates." To the ancient alchemist, the hermetic principle of vibration gave them the power to conquer natural phenomena in various ways and manifest at will. It is said that once students fully understand the principle of vibration, they have grasped the scepter of power. Ancient Hermetic masters understood the power of vibration, and many modern visionaries also understood its power. Nikola Tesla stated, "If one wants to understand the universe, think in terms of energy, frequency, and vibration." We are well on our way to understanding the universe so let's continue.

At the quantum level, subatomic particles that form all matter, physical and metaphysical, move back and forth in cycles in a wave-like motion to produce this vibration. This motion is called the motion of the universe and is where the concept of time comes from. We discuss this in detail in Chapter 5.

Seven layers comprise the human body system, ranging from etheric down to dense matter. All these body layers are composed of vibrating subatomic particles that create magnificent amounts of energy. One's consciousness is vibrational, but so is the physical body; everything a human is made of comes down to its vibration.

Vibration has three characteristics: how far a vibration can travel (amplitude), how fast it can travel (frequency), and the speed at which it travels (acceleration). The strength of a vibration is related to its amplitude and frequency, and per the universal law of resonance, the strongest vibration is always dominant. Therefore, if different vibrations are forced into the same space simultaneously, the dominant vibration will tune the surrounding vibrations to match it.

We will focus primarily here on the frequency part of vibration or its speed. Though there are unlimited universal vibrational speeds, we will condense these to only two, slow and fast. Slow and fast vibrations are referred to as low and high vibrations in spiritual terms.

High-vibrational energy resonates faster, the energy is more positive, and the data within the energy is very structured and advanced. This is the type of energy that nature and life are composed of. Therefore, fast or high-vibrating energy manifests itself as the six pillars of the divine.

1) Love
2) Peace
3) Joy
4) Health
5) Abundance
6) Freedom

In contrast, low vibrational energy resonates at a slower frequency, and the energy is more negative. The data within the energy is less structured and contains more entropy. It is not sustainable and is always in a state of decline.

This low-vibrational energy is the energy of the third-dimensional Matrix, which is an artificial construct. This type of energy is the opposite of beautiful and natural, and it does not support sentient life.

Low vibes manifest as the six pillars of the non-divine.

1) Pain/Suffering/Sickness/Toxicity
2) Hate
3) Fear
4) Bondage/Poverty
5) Depression
6) Anxiety

Conscious beings know instantly by their senses and emotions whether any vibration is high or low. High vibes are pleasant to the senses and feel good to the emotions. Low vibes are unpleasant to the senses, and they feel bad to the emotions.

Unconscious beings are not so aware of how vibrations affect them, nor are they in control of how they vibrate, but conscious beings, on the other hand, certainly are. Conscious beings know they control the vibrations that affect them, not the other way around. They also know they can make a free-will choice of whether to vibrate high or low. Lastly, they understand the procedures on how to modulate this vibration accordingly.

Since low-vibrational energies only manifest unpleasant things, there is only one intelligent and beneficial choice among vibrations, vibrate high! A simple but primary Pleiadian teaching to humanity says, "Always vibrate high, for this is the goal of life."

Reaching and maintaining a high vibration is a foundational requirement for all conscious evolution and ascension. All Base Twelve Universal Systems operate by vibration, and as any of these systems vibrate faster (higher), they function at more advanced levels.

The main question is, how does one raise their vibration and maintain a steady high vibe? We discuss this in detail in our Ascension Chapter.

Another important universal principle to master, related to vibration, is the law of attraction.
This law says, "energy vibrating at a certain frequency attracts other energies that resonate at the same frequency." Like energies always attracts like energies in this universe, and different energy vibrations always repel each other. In Chapter twelve on manifesting, we discuss using this energy attraction to your advantage.
If one wants to know where they are vibrating, they need only look at what they attract into their life. One may be attracting wonderful things in most areas but then, in one area, attracting something which doesn't seem to resonate. The hard truth is that one thing does resonate, or it

would not be here, so be assured one brought it into their life, themselves. If something not-so-nice showed up in one's high-vibe world. They did not manifest it to teach themselves a lesson, and the universe is also not trying to teach them; they brought the lower energy into their life simply because some part of them resonated with it and attracted it. The fact that it keeps showing up signifies that it needs to be dealt with and transmuted into higher energy.

The conscious and corrective work here is to examine the attracted energy and look deeper into one's self to see what part of one resonates that way. At first, there is usually denial about this; however, if one is ready for a change and looks deep enough, one will find the answer. This soul searching is the introspection, healing, and purging of lower energies required for conscious evolution. We discuss this more in our Ascension Chapter.

Everything one does affects their vibration. One's vibrational energy is sacred and should be treated as such. This energy is one's life force, and one must manage this personal energy wisely. We understand that becoming an expert in high vibrations takes much work, practice, and time. Until one reaches the level where they have transcended all lower energies, safeguarding one's vibrational energy along the way is good practice. Setting safe, energetic boundaries against low-vibrational people, places, and things can help protect and cultivate a high frequency.

The ancient writings of Earth say, *"When one has a negative emotional reaction to something, they create hell, first inside the body and then all around the body."* This teaching further says, *"When one can pause and inject understanding and love into the situation and not react, they create heaven, first inside the body and then all around it."*

Since all things in the universe, including living beings, are entangled at the quantum level, every being you encounter in life is a mirror reflecting your energy to you. When one senses any low-vibrational energy reflected toward them, it feels unpleasant, and usually, they mistakenly think it is coming from the other person. As a result, the one looking in the mirror often becomes triggered emotionally and has an unconscious negative reaction aimed at the other being. This triggering of one's emotions is the work of the universe to create awareness of energies that need to be transmuted. The triggered one can only subdue their negative reactions by transmuting the presented low-vibe energy into love. This universal mirroring and triggering will happen in cycles until the energy is transmuted.

The universe knows best what one needs, and though it may seem like tough love, it has the highest loving purpose. Here is where mastery is required; the one that mirrors and triggers you the most will usually come in the form of your most intimate partner, referred to as a twin flame. Keep in mind that there are several different types of twin flames, and the one you get is the one that most matches your vibration and the one you need most at that moment. These twin loves are no less than angels in disguise and are there to heal you, regardless. This universal mirroring and triggering process is the law of attraction at its finest and is worthy of understanding. A master of vibrations knows what is happening in this mirroring and triggering process, so instead of blaming or attacking the other person, they hold their peace, turn inward, and examine their energy.

The more one attunes their vibration; the more one sees how vibes affect all experiences. The more one understands and works with their vibration, the more one repels energetic realities that do not resonate. They will eventually master steadily holding a high vibration regardless of outside influence. The vibrational master becomes the silent observer of things, allowing them to be just as they are, without judgment or attachment. Our Ascension chapter discusses transmuting all low-vibrational energy from one's being.

A great evolution of consciousness is taking place on planet Earth, and many awakened starseeds know how important it is to maintain a high personal vibration. These light beings know that consciousness is vibration, and when this vibration speeds up, consciousness levels expand, opening up new realities and possibilities.

The ascending being learns they do not need to save the world. In time, they realize that true world transformation begins at the vibrational level, so they start correctly placing their energetic focus on themselves and begin this transformation inside. They do not focus on themselves egoically but in a healthy, self-respecting, loving way. They know one must nurture their vibrational energy field; otherwise, they could never truly serve others.

The master knows that all things in this universe are connected and entangled energetically, and when one changes self, they change the whole world. When one raises their vibration, one raises the collective's vibration and consciousness, not just on Earth but across the vastness of the cosmos. This is the great power of vibration.

Chapter 3: Light

If one asks, "What is light?" One could receive several different answers.

In physics, light is electromagnetic radiation, described as a stream of particles (photons), each traveling in a wave-like pattern, carrying energy and moving at the speed of light through space. One can see some of this light but not all of it.

In quantum physics, light appears to act like waves when you're not watching but acts like particles when you are watching, so it's hard to know exactly what you are seeing. In quantum physics, the consciousness observing the light determines what light is.

To the everyday person, light is something important that illuminates the world so they can see.

We think a better understanding of light is given by the spiritual master who understands light to represent the divine. Masters of light know that light is everything that exists. It allows one to see around them in the everyday world but also allows them to see into other realms. The master knows it's about seeing in a higher way by being aware and conscious.

The Pleiadians call light information.
Light is the informational field that makes up the entire universe.

A primary Pleiadian teaching says, *"Light is information, and darkness is the lack of information."*

A wealth of sacred knowledge is held within this one statement about the nature of the universe itself and humankind's true history and current state of affairs.
When one is in the dark, they have no access to information. Therefore, another term to describe

darkness is the word 'hidden.' When someone is in darkness, the light of information is hidden and withheld.

The first modern Earth humans were created 350,000 years ago by advanced geneticists from the Sirius star system. These first Earth humans were created to intentionally have lower levels of consciousness and ability so they could be easily controlled and work for their creators.

Though a perfected twelve-stranded DNA template was used in this creation process, ten of humanity's twelve primary DNA strands were intently left in dormant mode, and only the first two survival DNA strands were left in place. Modern humanity's DNA was unplugged initially, and they were plunged into darkness with no information. They had no awareness of what had happened to them, which is the ultimate state of unconsciousness.

The good news is that when the ten human DNA strands were deactivated, the strands were left inside the human body. These dormant DNA strands can be re-activated using the principles and methods listed in this book.

When a DNA strand is active, universal light flows through it, and this light information is made available to the consciousness that inhabits the body. Read more about DNA in Chapter 8.

Twelve primary light bands in this universe make up the EM (Electromagnetic) Spectrum. Each of these twelve bands corresponds vibrationally to the twelve primary states of consciousness, the twelve chakras, the twelve primary DNA strands, and the twelve dimensions. Other names for this electromagnetic light are scalar energy, tachyon energy, and cosmic radiant energy, understood and demonstrated by Nikola Tesla. All things are manifested by this light, including the human body. If a human body becomes damaged, it can be quickly rebuilt from a holographic projection of the original DNA template onto the damaged area.

These twelve bands or frequencies of light are composed of intelligent packets of vibrational information that emanate from the quantum field. These data packets are very structured bits of information programmed to operate every aspect of the universe. The blueprint of life itself, all processes of physics and metaphysics, and the knowledge and history of all things are encoded within this light. The information contained in this light is decoded solely by consciousness. Remember **Pleiadian tenant number one,** *"For anything to exist, consciousness is required!"*

The structured energy patterns encoded within these light bands are often called light codes by Earth starseeds. When put together in a series, light codes are called light language. Conscious beings are light receptacles that can receive and interpret this language of light, store it in the body's cells and anchor it into the crystal grid of planet Earth for others to access. Reiki is the Earth's primary spiritual energy modality, and it is based on the transmission of light codes. When activated into one's awareness by meditation, light codes bring one into a deeper embodied, resonate understanding of how the universe works. These sacred light patterns also trigger cellular remembrance of the whole picture and about who one is at the individual soul level.

The most influential band of universal light resonates in the twelfth dimension. This twelfth-dimensional light band contains photons with an energy above 2 PeV and is nothing short of a cosmic nuclear accelerator. The Pleiadians call this twelfth-dimensional light 'The great central sun' or source energy.

Twelfth-dimensional source light is transduced from the primary star at the twelfth dimension down through the universe until it reaches a second sun located in the core of the milky way galaxy, in the fifth-dimensional level of the universe.

This Sun or star in the core of the milky way galaxy has been called a black hole, an exotic star, the invisible sun, the black sun, and the central sun. Light emitted from this central sun interacts with Earth's sun, which ejects this high-vibrational light towards the Earth as solar flares and coronal mass ejections.

The Pleiadians call this fifth-dimensional light gamma light. Gamma light has much lower power than high-energy gamma rays and is the perfect energy for cultivating life on Earth.

Gamma is the frequency of light that resonates in the range of 40-100 hertz and corresponds vibrationally to the fifth dimension, the fifth state of consciousness (gamma consciousness), the fifth chakra portal (throat chakra), and the fifth primary strand of DNA.

When the fifth DNA strand is activated by gamma light, it connects energetically back into the fifth chakra portal, allowing the gamma consciousness to be attained. The gamma state of consciousness decodes and manifests itself as the outwardly perceived reality of the fifth dimension.

If one notices, 'light' seems important in ascension, awakening, and conscious evolution. After 350,000 years of darkness on Earth, the planet is moving back into an area of the cosmos where high vibrational central sun rays are reaching the Earth again.

As these cosmic light rays impact the surface of planet Earth, exotic particles penetrate the auric energy field of the human body vessel at speeds of nearly two million mph. They are then transported into every cell of the body. Gamma light particles have a well-defined geometric lattice structure that imprints the body's cells, transforming them into crystalline structures. This crystalline imprinting and morphing of the cells is the formation of the light body. We discuss the light body in our Ascension Chapter.

As more and more of this high-vibrational, fifth-dimensional light reaches Earth, it triggers a biological evolution. These cosmic rays are entering the crystalline Earth at much higher levels now, discharging an ionizing type of radiation that neutralizes, cleans, recodes, energizes, transforms, and rebuilds DNA, allowing all living systems to expand and breathe in more light.

Major cosmic cycles are beginning anew, allowing more and more cosmic light to reach Earth. The planet is also moving deeper into the photon belt, where higher levels of cosmic rays are naturally flowing into Earth. Benevolent light forces are doing their part to aid humanity's conscious evolution by deflecting the right amounts of gamma light toward the planet.

This fifth-dimensional light is triggering a magnificent expansion of consciousness on Earth. Humanity is waking up, one by one, from a long slumber as the dawning light shines in their eyes. The ancients foretold the great awakening of human consciousness and predicted it to happen in this modern time when the light of 'The great sun' would return and shine again on the Earth.

You came to Earth intently for the primary purpose of holding high-vibrational light in your body on behalf of all humanity. You are receiving and holding this light in your cells until the others can hold it for themselves. For this great work, we thank you and give you the highest honor. Glorious light has indeed come into this world, and since you are the holder of the light, you have become the light. Therefore, you are the light of the world.

Chapter 4: Sound

"In the beginning, the primordial sound manifested itself as all creation. It is the logos, the eternal and unchanging truth. The liberating sound spoke from the stillness that reconciles the human with the divine. "
The Pleiadians

The Rishis of ancient Vedic tradition believed that man was made of sound and light. They believed that the vibrations released by certain types of sound opened dimensional doors to higher consciousness causing a powerful spiritual shift in an individual's life.

Sound is a primary aspect of vibratory consciousness and is fundamental to the universal creation process.

Sound waves organize themselves into complex, uniform geometric patterns that form the platonic solids of all created matter. The science of cymatics illustrates how sound waves vibrating at different frequencies create the sacred geometry and framework of the material world.

All living beings are receptive to and inclined to reverberate with resonating sound tones. Furthermore, since a state of consciousness falls within a specific frequency range, one can alter their consciousness by tuning it to the vibration of a sound.

Sound waves such as harmonious music, words, chants, tones, mantras, and prayers are very effective tools for increasing one's internal vibration and inducing a state of balance and harmony in the mind and body.

Sound has a direct effect on the internal process of ascension. When a DNA strand is exposed to high vibrational sound frequencies, it starts resonating much like a tuning fork and will match the frequency of the sound. When any of the twelve primary DNA strands is resonating at its peak resonance, it moves into an active state, and the strand reconnects to its corresponding chakra port. As discussed in our DNA Chapter, when a DNA strand becomes active and reconnects to its chakra port, it performs much like a crystalline fiber optic cable where pure universal light begins flowing through the strand and moves through every cell of the body.

This influx of high-vibrational light flowing through the body excites a cell's subatomic particles causing them to move into a high spin state. The body becomes more energy than matter at this point, activating the crystalline light body of the ascension.

Many cultures throughout the ages have practiced sound healing therapy, and in today's modern world, sound therapy is fast becoming an accepted form of healing for the mind and body. The auric energy field, the Merkaba that surrounds the physical body, can be disrupted and knocked out of kilter by stress. Sound wave therapy can instantly realign this geometric field of life to its optimal state. Since this etheric body is where all healing begins, all body systems begin functioning at optimal levels when it is balanced harmonically with sound, back to the natural state.

The ancient, advanced civilizations of Earth understood the power of sound. They knew the harmonics and geometry of sound produced a state of negative mass which has an anti-gravity effect on matter. These ancient masters not only used sound waves to levitate and move 100-ton megalithic stones but also knew that certain frequencies affect natural phenomena and could unlock dimensional gates. These spiritual masters of sound could perform all sorts of what would be called magic today.

The emerald tablets passed down from Great Atlantis are a prime example of this and list specific words, tones, chants, and mantras that give one supernatural ability. The ancient Hindus teach that every word and syllable of the sacred Veda texts are literal divine words of power, and as they are uttered, the laws of nature are affected. These sacred power words profoundly affect one's state of consciousness.

The Hathors of ancient Egypt, a group of female priestesses, descendants from ancient Lemuria, known as the Seven Sisters of the Pleiades, were master healers in the grand crystal temples of those days. The primary method of healing used by these priestesses was sound vibrations. Atlantean and Egyptian temple healings involved chanting, toning, breathwork, and hi-tech, vibrating sound instruments.

In Chapter 12, we teach about the subconscious mind or right brain, which is directly connected to universal superconsciousness. One of the few ways to gain programming access to this super mind is by merging it with the left brain creating whole-brain coherence. Whole-brain coherence can be achieved in minutes using particular sound tones called binaural beats. There are many wonderful frequencies of sound and music; however, it just so happens that 40-hertz gamma frequency tones have a magical quality. 40-hertz gamma sound resonates with and is the sound of the fifth dimension. This 40-hertz fifth-dimensional sound produces optimal human learning ability, improved memory, verbal recall, and reaction time.

"The fastest way to raise one's vibration is to listen to high vibrational music."
The Pleiadians

Music was never invented or discovered by anyone, at any point, in the known history of the universe. It has simply just been there the whole time as a creative aspect of universal expression. Nevertheless, certain tones, patterns in different types of music, and certain repetitive rhythms can be very attractive to our vibrational bodies. Something magical happens inside when one sits back with a powerful and high-vibe piece of music in their headset. We challenge you to give it a try and take notice of how you begin to feel. After some repetitive listening to high-vibe music that moves the soul, one will feel this positive resonance in the very cells of their body. At that moment, one will automatically increase their spiritual strength and physical immunity by default.

When the body is exposed to high-vibrational music, DNA activates, opening the body's energy channels and allowing in higher energies. These higher energies trigger the release of dopamine, serotonin, oxytocin, and endorphins into the bloodstream, producing powerful emotions of awe and bliss. These wonderous feelings are the amazing effect of divine sound flowing through the central nervous system.

Furthermore, one has an emotional layer in the layered body system; when the right vibe is present, this body activates. Emotions connect one to the non-physical body, which gives direct access to source energy. When one feels deep positive emotions, they are connected directly to higher consciousness and are in the God state. Many beings in the third-dimensional matrix are taught not to feel or express their emotions, but we say you must feel them fully to become the ascended master.

Listening to certain drumming and beat sessions will also create elevated states of consciousness. After exposure to steady rhythmic beats, just like a tuning fork, the body begins to vibrate to match the beat of the music. Be selective when choosing drum and beat music; ensure the rhythm feels good.

Ancient musical styles have a stronger effect on one's state of consciousness because the cellular memory of those ancient times is triggered and unlocked by this type of music. This ancient musical style was performed in grand crystal temples of Earth's past, and if it seems very attractive and familiar to you, it's because, in those days, you played, listened to, and danced to this exotic form of music.

So, how does one know if a piece of music is high-vibe music? First, ask yourself, "How does it make you feel? Does it move your soul? Does it make you want to move physically and dance? Can you listen to it repeatedly in a loop and not grow tired of it?" If you answered yes to these questions, it is high-vibe music. Lastly, ask yourself, "What kind of music turns you on?" and that's the best starting place.

Someone asked, "Is rock and roll ok for a spiritual person?" The Pleiadian answer is, "Yes, of course, it is." The musicians that create awesome songs, including rock and roll, are doing it from a higher state of creative consciousness. It is irrelevant to the style or the genre of music as long as it elevates one's being.

Good Headphones are a must. Make sure you have enough volume and that you can feel a super bass and drumbeat.

We suggest that you begin searching for this high-vibe music, and in these modern times, you can easily create a super-vibe playlist that can elevate you at any time. Then, when your super-vibe playlist is ready, play it in your headset, crank it up, and start ascending.

Vocal singing is a form of sound vibration where one produces musical tones with the voice. Singing is simply uttering words in musical tones and with musical inflections and modulations. The human being is divinely equipped to create musical tones vocally, which in turn not only stimulates one's DNA but also stimulates the DNA of other living beings raising their vibrational level. As part of the divine plan of sound, humans can combine vocal singing with unlimited musical instrument tones to create epic masterpieces of sound and resonance. Did you know a being that could not sing so well in the third dimension but who now has an open throat chakra will be able to sing in a beautiful and perfected way?

Lastly and most importantly is the power of language and the spoken word. Spoken words are the fuel that drives all of creation. As one will see in our Manifesting Chapter, thinking of things and words is the beginning level of manifestation; however, decreeing a thing intently and with power by the spoken word guarantees manifestation.

"A thing that is decreed is so."
The Pleiadians

One will get to the point where they can decree, "let there be light," and it shall be so.

The awesome power of words must be clearly understood for one to progress along their spiritual journey. Science has shown a direct correlation between DNA and language; the spoken word can edit the genetic code directly.

The ancients knew that words are a literal form of magic and that when one speaks, they cast a spell which is the meaning and function behind the word 'spelling.'

Of course, the universal law behind this magic scientifically explains that words are forms of geometric sound energy that manifest as the material world.

The phonetic sound of the words is a very important part of their power, but the energy and intent behind the words are even more important. Certain words and the intent behind them can be used to bless, and words can be used negatively to create what might be called cursing words. Therefore, it is critical in one's expansion of conscious awareness to take careful notice of the words one speaks each day. This applies to words spoken over others and the words one speaks over themselves. Positive affirmations are among the most powerful energy tools for quickly improving one's state of being and manifesting the desired reality. We discuss affirmations in our Manifesting Chapter.

At this time on Earth, humanity is moving from third to fifth-dimensional reality. Every dimension has a corresponding and resonating chakra portal that allows access to that dimension. The fifth chakra, the throat chakra, is the key focal point for modern planet Earth because this chakra portal is the doorway into the fifth dimension.

Before a being becomes enlightened, they live in a lower state of unconsciousness. In this state, one lives in an illusion, held in the lower world by their level of truth. One is in the dark at that stage with no information, and no light of truth is shining on them.

Regarding sound and speaking, since one's throat was energetically closed in the lower state of consciousness, one had difficulty speaking and living their inner truth, often just going along with everyone else's truths.

After experiencing several life-changing events, one finally begins to stir awake, moving up through the seven layers of the fourth dimension. They have opened all their lower energy chakras, including an expanded new heart, and they are ready to enter the kingdom of heaven. The next chakra doorway one must open on the Ascension ladder is number five, the throat chakra. As a spiritual being, one realizes the importance and power of an open heart chakra; however, one must consider that the throat chakra is one level above the heart and resonates higher than the heart.

While awakening occurs in many subtle levels through each dimension, one of the most profound levels occurs as one arrives at the fifth dimension.

This is when a spiritual being finally grows up.

It is when they reach their first level of maturity.

It is when the higher wisdom comes.

It is when great power comes.

It's when things start going right for the first time.

It is when one becomes the master.

What is the cause behind this profound change and mastery?

The fifth chakra, the throat chakra, is the chakra of truth. When one opens this doorway to the fifth dimension and fifth-dimensional light starts rushing into the light body; one begins to speak their inner truth for the first time. As one goes forth decreeing this truth, they begin living their truth. One then becomes the truth, and they can say, "I am the truth." The truth is the light, and as one moves forward on their journey, they become the light that walks among humanity in this world. Finally, at the peak of their spiritual journey, they speak about the kingdom of light and begin demonstrating this fifth-dimensional kingdom before humanity. One then becomes 'The way' to the kingdom of light and to God for all others to follow.

*"You are the way, the truth, and the light for all humanity."***The Pleiadians**

Chapter 5: Time

"If not now, when?"
The Pleiadians

To realize the true nature of time is to become a master of time.

Time is a big deal on Earth, and there is never enough of it. It is a cardinal sin not to be on time in the third-dimensional matrix. Life in the physical realm is strictly organized and made more efficient by adhering to the agreed-upon time system, which is measured down to the second by clocks and calendars. This adherence to Earth time can create stress as one constantly watches the clock and calendar to ensure they're on time. We have even heard the phrase, "money is time, and time is money." Although these kinds of time may be beneficial for organizing and structuring one's life on Earth, this 'time' is only a mental and illusionary concept that has nothing to do with the reality of time.

Some may ask the following questions about time, "If Earth time is only an illusionary concept, why does the body age, and why does an older adult often pray for more time to live?"
Many wish they could spend more time doing the things they love, and when they do not do this, there is often much regret later. Similarly, many wish they could spend more time just being in the presence of those they love dearly, and when this isn't accomplished, again, there is often much regret later. How can something that is not real be so precious and desired?

A master of time learns to conquer time. On one's evolutionary journey towards higher consciousness, one eventually transcends the lower laws and gains control over time, not the other way around. At that point, one is no longer bound by time and begins to operate outside of its restrictions. When one understands the true nature of time, one realizes they are eternal and have all the time in the universe. They become a master of time. Masters of time are aware that Earth time is an illusion and that the mental concepts of past and future are also an illusion. The master of time is aware that in the ultimate sublime reality, the body doesn't age; nothing does. The time master knows that body aging is simply the deterioration of body cells, which can be prevented and has nothing to do with time. The master of time does only what they love and are always near their loved ones. A master of time has no regrets.

The beings of the Earth say time passes, but time is not an object that can pass or move anywhere. They say time flows, but time is not fluid, so it cannot flow. Therefore, time doesn't pass through or by anything. Likewise, nothing passes or moves through time because time is not a thing or field that something can move through.

We said that the third-dimensional Earth concept of time and the past and future are illusions; however, we did not say that time was an illusion. There is a real-time, and you are about to become the master of it.

This real-time does not advance in a line or a cycle. It doesn't do anything; it just is. It is invariant, eternal, and still and cannot be measured.

This real-time of the universe is called the eternal now moment. The now moment is the only time and the only moment of reality. Reality itself cannot exist unless it exists now.

Consciousness itself exists only in the now moment, and this is its very nature. Therefore, to be conscious is to be aware of the now moment.

The ultimate knowledge and skill of the master of time are to bring full focus and conscious awareness into the present moment. The master knows that the magic of life and the universe only occur in this state. This now-focused awareness is called presence or being present and is divine.

There is great power within the moment, and the goal is to keep one's focus on it as much as possible. In this moment of presence, all things become as they truly are, at one. These masters of time often use a candle flame as their now-moment focal point to keep their awareness anchored to this only true time. After much practice of this 'now' focus, one eventually masters the art of staying present, and their consciousness levels are greatly elevated.

Here is a valuable general technique one can practice each day to perfect their mastery of time. Everyday existence on Earth can be very distracting so when the mind trails away into the illusionary past or the future, practice becoming aware this is happening, and when you notice it, say the trigger word 'now' to yourself abruptly. Then, at that second, intently bring all your conscious awareness into the present moment and practice maintaining this presence.

Thinking about the pleasant memories of the past and dreaming of the future is a normal part of life. However, when one tries to exist in a sustained way in either of these non-realities, one's required energy for physicality begins to dissipate. This is because if one constantly lives in the past or the future mentally, they are not grounded in the only reality of now, where material things manifest. Energy flows where consciousness goes, so if consciousness moves out of the now reality frame, one's physical being is no longer receiving the required observance energy it needs to stay manifested. So, where is your local, physical existence while the mind wanders into the non-reality of the past or future? It's as if one's local self doesn't seem to exist during these false time trips. Also, notice that your immediate local existence came back as soon as your consciousness came back and observed all of it.

The Pleiadians

To operate at optimal universal power and energy levels and for life to unfold at its fullest, one must keep one's consciousness focused on the now, the only reality of time.

Now is the only time, even in physics; now is when you exist and the only time you can exist. Therefore, all existence is in an eternal state of being that only occurs in the present moment. This moment has no beginning and no end. It is always and forever.

What about time travel to the past and future? If now is the only time that exists and the past and future are only mental concepts, how can time travel be possible?

One might say, "I am convinced that secret groups on Earth and advanced galactic civilizations have already achieved time travel."

If one suspects this, they are correct!

We must clear up an important issue before we speak about travel through time.

The phrase' time travel' is not the correct phrase for describing travel to the past, the future, or the present, for that matter. This phrase is quite misleading because one cannot travel through time. As we said, time is not something one can travel through; furthermore, as we will see in our Space chapter, one does not travel anywhere. A better word than 'travel' might be 'shift.'

Regardless, there is a real past and future, and one can shift into either of these. It's just that the wrong labels and descriptions are used to describe the past and future.

The very real past and future are not times but are referred to as timelines and can be described as alternate realities.

If you ask someone to describe what a past time was like, for example, the year 1800, most will begin describing the 1800 clothing style or mention that folks lived in log homes and used horses and wagons for transportation. Likewise, if you could obtain a first-hand description of the year 3035, one will most likely describe the technology used in that future year and tell you how futuristic things looked. But, if you noticed, nothing in these descriptions of the past and future describes time.

Time is about rates of change and events occurring and is not really about time.

An alternate timeline is a different version of reality composed of different events and rates of change and often includes an illusionary time and date stamp. Only the outwardly perceived scene changes when an alternate reality is observed and manifested, not the time.

These timelines are isolated and separated from each other by their vibrational resonance. All of these infinite parallel timelines or alternate realities are occurring right now, in the present moment. These alternate realities are sub-levels of vibration contained within the twelve dimensions of this universe.

Think of these timelines more like individual film frames or photo snapshots of every reality that exists and will ever exist in this universe. Let's call these frames 'reality frames'. Now picture these snapshots or frames placed in one tall stack that reaches from the bottom to the top of the universe. The stack itself is the now moment (time), and each frame is a different snapshot of the infinite realities that make up what may be perceived as the past and future. One billion years ago, the year 1900, and the year 3050 are all occurring now in their own reality frame. Each of these frames exists at a different and specific vibrational frequency, and no two frames are composed of the same information. The vibrational information within a frame can be decoded, projected, and manifested as the now-time reality by a resonant conscious observer. Consciousness projection works much like video player software that, by default, plays these frames in order, in forward motion in a steady live-streaming way.

Masters of time are the creators and manifesters of time. By default, during the waking state of consciousness, the beta state, one does very little or no shifting through time-reality frames, and one usually only manifests time with little or no change in this time being perceived. One is already shifting constantly and instantly into alternate time realities. Still, they are only shifting to immediate adjacent near-identical frames, where the frames share more data with the now moment. In higher consciousness states, however, one can instantly shift into more complex alternate reality frames that share very little common data with the now moment. An example of these more complex frames might be the years 9000 BC or 6035. Even so, the successful time-jumper, the observer, still experiences these very different reality frames as the now moment.

Time Travel (Time-Line Jumping).

In various secret projects, jumping across timelines using technology was achieved on Earth nearly 80 years ago.

For example, in the Philadelphia Experiment of 1943, U.S. naval scientists created a space-time portal by combining gravity and electromagnetism into one field. Giant coils for generating this field were placed around a navy ship loaded with sailors. Though the experiment worked, at this early stage of Earth technology, the space-time jump resulted in casualties and re-materialization problems. As a result, the project was shelved after ending in tragedy.

The Philadelphia Project was a precursor to The Montauk Project of 1983 that involved integrating human consciousness with a computerized space-time algorithm and amplifying and broadcasting the output. This Project was an artificial re-creation and boosting of the natural manifestation process of consciousness. Unfortunately, though it worked to shift many young, unwilling participants into alternate space-time realities, this project created some nightmares and was also terminated after it ended in tragedy.

DARPA Project, Pegasus was another secret project where a space-time tunnel was successfully opened, allowing a jump to alternate timelines and back. The time portal in this project was a "shimmering curtain of radiant energy projected between two elliptical booms." The amazing technology used in this timeline-jumping project is attributed to Nikola Tesla.

Shifting to past and future timelines have also been achieved in secret projects naturally, using human consciousness. This was accomplished in The Gateway Project in 1983. This timeline-shifting project successfully worked by using heightened levels of consciousness to interact with the universal hologram of time and space in a process called 'space-time transcendence.' This interaction with universal reality frames was combined with a deep meditative out-of-body experience for the shifting part. In modern times, The Gateway Project documentation has been declassified. Here is a synopsis partly derived from this documentation that illustrates how natural conscious timeline jumping can be achieved.

Shifting or jumping onto an alternate timeline is as easy as changing one's resonance to match the desired reality frame of that timeline. This is achieved via deep meditation, energetic focus, and an out-of-body experience. However, just because it's done this way naturally doesn't mean it is not a real experience with tangible results.

One must first move into the alpha state of consciousness to successfully jump timelines during meditation. Certain alpha-level binaural beats can be used to make reaching this state easier. The jump scene must also be experienced as real as possible to match resonance with a desired timeline reality frame. This is done by intensely focusing on the chosen reality frame and achieving a heightened sensory awareness. All the senses must fully perceive the jump scene because consciousness uses the senses to build the energetic template for the reality it is about to manifest.

Furthermore, the desired reality frame must be experienced 'now' because this is the only time reality can exist. One is ready to jump when it becomes impossible to differentiate the desired alternate reality frame from the present. When the scene from the perceived future or past becomes the perceived now reality, one will feel as if one has been here before, and indeed, one has. The jump is achieved as a subtle out-of-body shift into the new desired reality frame or timeline. Timeline shifting requires a thorough understanding of the topics discussed here, a high level of conscious mastery, and, just like anything, it can take some practice before one is successful.

What are the implications of timeline shifting? Reality frames are universal constants that do not and cannot change, and the observer (the timeline jumper) certainly cannot change a reality frame. Therefore, simply shifting to these alternate timelines creates a brand-new timeline and a new present from the observer's perspective.

Besides creating a different perceived reality for oneself, there are no implications of timeline jumping or paradoxes.

A related phenomenon involving time is the ability to slow it down or speed it up.

Since we have deduced that time is only a mental construct and what we think of as time is the rate of change of things, instead of slowing down or speeding up time, one would be slowing down or speeding up the rate of change of things around them.

It turns out that, yes, this can be done, and one does it with consciousness, of course. Heightened consciousness levels can contract and expand space-time. The Lambda state of consciousness is triggered when one perceives danger, where time seems to slow to a crawl, and there is a clear perception of this slowdown occurring around you. This state of being is a survival state designed for physical protection and preservation. With time slowed down and you moving at normal speed, you have time to make some quick adjustments and protect yourself before impending danger impacts the body. Beings that have achieved this slowed-down state say the pixels of reality are also transformed into ultra-HD quality so one can easily notice every detail. Though this slowdown of so-called time usually only happens when danger flies in one's face, it is possible to reach this state in meditation. Master, martial artists, can slow down everything that is moving around them while in battle so they can successfully counteract every movement of their enemy in plenty of time. Many have described a related experience during heightened levels of consciousness when danger is near, where consciousness not only slows down but seems to split into multiple versions of itself that can view a dangerous scene from different angles allowing the observer to see the best route away from the danger.

What about speeding up the rate of change of matter around you, aka time?

You've heard the phrase; time flies by. Have you ever had an experience of bliss where there was great peace and no cares or worries, where you felt the timelessness of now, and your whole life became just one moment? Many have described the time spent suspended in this state as many hours passing, but after this experience, no time seemed to have passed.

Either way, all the change that one is aware of around them, perceived as time passing, is occurring now, always.

As one's consciousness becomes more evolved, one creates more time, and the creator of time is the controller and master of time.

It is time to be free from time! Do away with the old mental construct of time and make your own

time. Make time for the beautiful now moments
of life.

Chapter 6: Space

"There is no out there, and the entire universe exists inside you."
The Pleiadians

In our time chapter, we discussed that the only real time is the eternal now moment, and since time and space are two sides of the same coin, space works the same way.

In the most sublime and true sense, the only place or space that exists in the universe is right here.

There is only one point of space, and it is the space around you that you are conscious of. This (here) space is singular, eternal, still, and does not move or change. There are not two or multiple spaces in the entire universe; there is only one.

Think of the word 'nowhere.' Nowhere is a combination of the words' now' and 'here' and this now and here time and space are the only reality. The reason it is called nowhere is that one cannot go anywhere. This is because there is nowhere to go. To make matters more restrictive, even if one could go somewhere, there is no time to get there. This may all sound a bit strange and philosophical at first; however, even though there is the perception of traveling between two points, places, or spaces, regardless of where one thinks they are going, they always remain here, in the only space that exists. 'Here' is the one true reality of space, and this one space exists only where conscious awareness exists.

The notion of one single space negates the concepts of distance and travel. There are no two points that one can travel between. Though it seems that on an everyday scale, things are found to exist in different places or locations, defined by coordinates and in relation to other things, all separated by distance. Furthermore, it seems that one can indeed travel between these separate things; however, just like everything else in the physical realm, things are never as they seem.

The principles of non-locality illustrate that the universe is non-local and that there are no places or spaces other than 'here.' Under the quantum mechanics uncertainty principle, particles lack properties, including precise location prior to measurement. Quantum energy particles that make up all matter can never be found or situated in any specific place because there is no such thing as a specific place. Because these particles of matter lack differentiating attributes, things do not reside at points, and space cannot support any localized structure. Points in space are indistinguishable and interchangeable, and one can no sooner pin down the exact position of a particle than one could plant a flag in the ocean.

The principle of non-locality also nullifies the concept of movement. Movement is another misunderstood part of classical physics because the only thing that moves in the universe is the oscillating vibrations of the quantum field, and consciousness is the highest form of this vibration.

If there is only one point in space, how could something move away from it to another point? One may be reasonably sure they stood up and walked into the next room; however, if they could look close enough, they would see that no material things moved, only consciousness moved. Imagine a character walking or running into a building in a video game. Is the character moving in reality? This is exactly the way the physical world of matter works. The entire perceived physical realm, including spaces, places, and movements, is a mass of vibrational information projected by and to consciousness holographically.

Lastly, the concept of duality and the separateness of anything is destroyed by the law of non-locality. Everything in the universe is intimately connected and entangled. Everything is one, and non-local phenomena are not "actions at a distance" but the universe displaying its grand oneness.

The quantum physics observer effect further illustrates that when a conscious observer isn't conscious of a thing (looking at it), it doesn't exist physically. Let's apply this observer effect to the adjacent room in one's home. It may seem a bit shocking at first; however, the quantum fact is that the next room in one's home that one is not consciously observing is not there, at least until their consciousness changes focus to it!

As you will learn in our Manifesting Chapter, every combination of all things already exists in the quantum field in an energetic waveform, including the adjacent room of your home. These energetic waves are called waves of probability. When a conscious observer focuses on one of these probable energy waves, the adjacent room, in this case, the energetic waveform collapses and is converted into the physical matter of the next room. When consciousness shifts onto or observes the next room, it is manifested holographically and can be perceived instantly.

This manifestation of and perceptional shift onto the adjacent room occurs with no time passing.

Notice we used the term 'shift' above instead of 'travel' just like in our Time Chapter because consciousness shifts; it doesn't travel.

As strange as it sounds, the people in the other room are also not there and do not show up until you encounter them. You are creating the room and the other people by observing them. This concept goes back to the fact that you are the sole creator of everything on planet Earth and the entire universe, and this is your divine creative power. There are no other people around until you physically observe and manifest them. There has always and only just been you, the one consciousness. One may ask, "If I am the only being in the universe, why are so many other people around? The answer is, "Because it's lonely at the top! You manifested all of them to keep you company!" You created this whole thing, and the goal is to see if you can remember how you did it all and to find out what you're really up to. What we can say for sure is, "You are indeed the most advanced being that we know of!"

All the other so-called conscious observing eyes are simply your eyes, and the entire universe is there only when an observer can say, "Yes, I see the universe out there." An observer is required for a physical universe to be manifested. The universe and the observer exist as a pair, and as we said, physical existence requires consciousness.

Though there is only one point of space (here), just like time, there are infinite parallel versions of the 'here' space, vibrating at different frequencies. These vibrational levels of space are manifested and projected holographically only by a conscious observer, and in fact, space-time itself is solely dependent on conscious awareness. These differently-vibrating holographic projections of space are perceived physically as separate and very real (other) places but are all existing right here in the only one space that exists.

So, what is real, then?

If you mean what is real physically, the answer is anything that consciousness perceives, but if you mean what is real at a more fundamental level, then the answer is only consciousness.

The next room in your house is very real, but only when you encounter or manifest it. At that point, the adjacent room becomes 'The here room.' The only reason it looks different than any other room in your home is that the energetic information that makes up the room is different.

But what makes the adjacent room in your house really look the way it does, and why does it generally always look the same? Consciousness has its way of making things stick holographically and physically. Since there is only one consciousness ultimately, the collective consciousness, if the builder of your home observed the room in your house, he manifested it first. His observing eyes are the same as yours. He certainly built the room, but this building process is just another form of manifesting, one nail and one board at a time. A deeper rule of manifesting matter is that once a thing is observed, its energetic probability factor increases and the next observer manifests it similarly. The more observance, the more a thing sticks and hangs around in the holographic physical matrix.

The same applies to other towns, other cities, other countries, other planets, or any space in the universe. If one is not observing it, there is no across-town or another place (space). These outward physical projections only appear holographically when they come into view of conscious awareness. When one observes each of these vibrational spaces, one manifests them, and they exist as a different vibrational version of the here space.

"If you notice, when you are there, you are here."
The Pleiadians

Like time, if all differently perceived places or spaces of the universe were on separate movie frames and placed in one stack, the stack would be the one point of space called 'here.' More interestingly, since space and time are ultimately the same, one could place the time and space stack of movie frames in one stack. These movie frames of space and time are all in the 'now' time and 'here' moment stack, which we will call the space-time stack. These movie frames represent reality frames, more commonly called alternate realities or parallel realities. Parallel realities are not to be confused with parallel universes, as this book refers to the one particular universe we find ourselves in at the moment, which is different from other universes.

Just as we described time-traveling as shifting vibrationally into other reality frames, shifting through so-called space, even across the galaxy instantly, is accomplished the same way. This shifting to alternate space realities is done in the most simple, automatic, and natural way in every moment of life by simply changing focus to the next room, city, or town. Adjacent space reality frames are nearly identical in composition and may only contain a few bits of quantum information that makes the frame different from its neighboring frames. Therefore, one instantly projects and manifests the external physical world by continuously live-streaming reality frames with no gaps between them as one observes them with consciousness. This instant manifesting is the default mode of consciousness for dealing with space, and this mode is active during normal beta waking consciousness.

Jumping to a more complex space reality frame where the information that makes up the frame is very different from one's current local space, such as the Alpha Centauri frame, for example, can be easily achieved. One could indeed jump through a stargate or wormhole using technology successfully developed on Earth in the 1940s to teleport to Alpha Centauri. Alternatively, one could do this naturally by simply raising and matching their frequency to the frequency of the desired parallel space reality.

These alternate vibrational versions of the here space are entangled with consciousness. Higher consciousness levels can contract space-time, collapsing any parallel space instantly into right here, around you. If you really think about this, you will notice that you would not be traveling anywhere or jumping, for that matter.

Again, since space and time are parts of the same whole, use the same procedure we discussed for timeline traveling to shift into the perfect new space. If you want to live in a paradise, then manifest the paradise around you.

Teleportation, aka 'space-reality shifting,' is a very real and scientific phenomenon, just like time travel, aka 'time-reality shifting,' and it can easily be achieved using a higher state of vibrational consciousness.

When you become proficient at attaining altered states of consciousness during deep meditation and mastery of the out-of-body experience, you will appear on the profoundly beautiful other worlds in this universe. You will show up because you are the creator of these worlds.

95

"Here is always real, wherever you are!"
The Pleiadians

Chapter 7: Dimensions

This universe has twelve primary dimensional levels, and each resonates faster than the level below. All twelve dimensions exist in the only time that exists, now, and the only space that exists, here. Dimensions are often thought of as higher and lower levels, like the floors of a building. Dimensions, however, are not arranged in an up or down or higher or lower fashion. Since dimensions are different frequency ranges, one dimension simply vibrates faster or slower than another. Using the one-through-twelve sequential numbering system, the lower the number, the slower the vibration. Dimension three would vibrate slower than dimension five, for example.

Dimensions are not physical; they are vibration bands measured in hertz frequency. These dimensional frequency ranges are universal constants that do not change.

Dimensions are separated from each other by protective frequency barriers that work like vibrational filters and only allow matching vibrational levels to enter that dimension.

Typically, one dimension has nothing in common with another as they are entirely separated realities. The only thing that multiple dimensions have in common with each other is the conscious awareness that exists within them. It works like this; one already exists in all twelve dimensions in the same space-time, the same space at the same time; however, one's consciousness must resonate with the frequency range of a specific dimension to be aware of and operate in that dimension.

The twelve dimensions of this universe correspond precisely with the twelve primary states of consciousness discussed in Chapter 1, and a dimension is simply a vibrational state of being.

The vibrational energy or light data that a dimension is composed of is very structured. Therefore, this dimensional information can be decoded by consciousness and perceived as an entirely different outward reality.

Currently, the dominant vibrational resonance among humanity falls within the third-dimensional range, which resonates between seven to nine hertz. This energy field is very "dense" and vibrates slowly. At this slow vibrational rate, one's consciousness manifests and perceives more solid structure than energy, and this slower/lower vibrational rate creates the dualism experienced in the third-dimensional realm. At this time in Earth's history, humanity's consciousness is evolving to the point where it will soon be able to perceive and function in a higher dimension right here on Earth.

Humanity has existed in the third dimension for the last 350,000 years. They were intentionally placed into this lower state of consciousness by their creators, who had an agenda to control and manipulate them for selfish and commercial reasons. The third dimension is only one level above survival consciousness. Anyone who resonates in this state of being has little or no awareness that any other or better reality exists.

The Pleiadians say, "It is time for humanity to evolve to a higher state of consciousness and the fifth dimension is the goal and focus."

As soon as an Earth human has any awakening, they immediately bump up in resonance to the fourth dimension. Again, all dimensions occur in the same space at the same time, so this newly awakened being would find themself aware of higher vibrating things while walking on the Earth. In time he would notice the lower levels of the fourth dimension resonate higher than the third dimension. Still, the first few levels of the fourth dimension are more-amplified versions of the nightmares that occur on third-dimensional Earth.

Most Earth beings who have awakened to the fourth dimension usually go all out to save the world from the negative things they have discovered. Still, a fourth-dimensional being is not yet a master. So, though their intentions are noble and good, they usually move forward, bringing attention to the evils on Earth, which manifests even more of these low-vibrational things.

Many fourth-dimensional beings are aligned with every political conspiracy on the planet; most are protesting, fighting, and pushing against the evils of the third dimension, giving these things serious focus and energy, which only manifests more of the same energy. The 'powers-that-were' who work hard to keep the vibration of humanity low know this, and they welcome this helpful activism. These world controllers know that humanity manifests what they see, so they ensure the not-so-nice stuff is placed right in front of Earth's collective consciousness every hour of every day via media.

As a fourth-dimensional being moves ever higher in vibration, they ultimately realize they cannot change anything in the external world directly and can only change themselves. They stop fighting evil the traditional way and learn to fight in a higher way. They learn to fight without fighting. They realize they will only be successful in making things better if they work to transform things energetically from the inside out. They stop trying to tear down the low-vibrating control matrix and instead work with their brothers and sisters to create a new matrix of light that vibrates much higher. This new way of being is where one begins to gain true power and prepares to move into the fifth dimension.

The fourth dimension is transitionary and serves as the perfect ascension training ground for the light beings of Earth to do their inner work toward conscious mastery.

There are seven sub-levels within the fourth dimension, and it is critical for the ascending being to intently jump in conscious vibration as fast as possible above the first three layers. All masters are aware that what is called 'hell' is simply the first few layers of the fourth dimension, specifically the first layer, the astral realm. Beings that left their bodies on Earth with strong traumas or unresolved negative energies and emotions can land in this realm. Since low vibrations cannot move into the higher realms, these beings become stuck in the astral realm until they choose to transmute their low-vibrational energy. A higher-vibrating light being or guide always presents a free-will opportunity for these stuck beings to choose light over darkness, transmuting their lower astral energy, crossing them over, above the astral realm, towards the higher light.

The good news is that any being on Earth who makes any reasonable effort to raise their vibration while in the body will already be resonating above these lower fourth-dimensional levels. An excellent way to think about the fourth dimension is that it is much like the third one, only amplified in power. The first layers of the fourth dimension are lower energies amplified, and the higher levels are higher energies amplified.

As one moves from the third dimension up through the levels of the fourth dimension, it is possible to vibrate high in most areas but still possess some low vibrations.

"A prince dressed in fine clothing was walking up a celestial stairway, arriving at the gates of a king's palace. Before the prince knocks on the gate for entry, he looks down and notices he is carrying a smelly trash bag full of garbage. The prince quickly remembered that before he left for the palace, his wife had asked him to drop the garbage in the bin along the way. "
The Pleiadians

If one has cleared most of their trauma energies but still carries that one old energy around they have not dealt with and transmuted like the trash bag analogy above, issues will arise. All vibrations in the fourth dimension are greatly amplified from the third-dimensional level, so any old uncleared trauma energy will continue to manifest negatively but will manifest much more powerfully.
The Pleiadians teach that as one ascends, one must clear out all low vibrational energy. Let's say

one is ascending well up into the fourth dimension, but they still ingest low-vibrational toxic food. This didn't seem to matter so much in the lower realms, but if one is resonating in the higher realms and does this, the lower energy is amplified many times and will manifest as great pain and problems in the body. Of course, these pains and problems are a message from the universe for one to correct the issue quickly.

The Pleiadians say, "The ascending being must take the universal law of vibration seriously, and what one could get away with before, they can no longer get away with in the higher realms."

All masters who have traveled dimensionally know there is a point at the very top of the fourth dimension, at the upper boundary of the seventh level, just before the fifth dimension, called the great void or the great chasm. One can think of making it to this point up the dimensional ladder, and they are standing there at the top edge of the fourth dimension. Imagine one standing at the edge of the grand canyon, with a massive cavern in front of them. They look across and see a beautiful celestial city on the other side called heaven, the fifth dimension. The only issue is that one successfully made it this far on their ascension journey, so why now is this great void present that one cannot cross to get to this heavenly city?

Here is why. This great void or chasm is the energetic barrier between the fourth and fifth dimensions. It keeps any vibrations that do not match from entering the fifth dimension. It is as if one needs a rocket to propel themselves across this great void, and this notion is not far from reality.

A being must attain a perfected level of love before entering the fifth dimension. Think of the being's etheric body, the Merkaba, as the vehicle or rocket for traveling across dimensions, and think of love as fuel for the rocket. There are primarily two scenarios that can happen here to get across this dimensional barrier. The first scenario is that one has expanded their fourth-dimensional energy center, the heart chakra, to the point where pure unconditional love has been achieved. This will be enough power to propel one's being across this great void. However, if one has gotten nearly there with the heart but is still standing on the fourth-dimensional side of the great chasm, one may combine their love with the love of another to achieve the power needed to cross the great void. The only other love that is powerful enough to get one across the chasm to the other side is a true twin flame love. These two twin flames would have ascended to this last level together in perfect unison, and their combined love is so powerful it can easily propel both of them as one unit, across the great void, through the veil, into the fifth dimension.

After much work to master one's state of being, one finally becomes pure love, truth, and light, penetrating heaven's veil.

The fifth dimension is where everything changes in a significant way for ascending beings. One transcends all lower things when one ascends past the lower fifth-dimensional boundary.

Even though there are seven unspeakably majestic dimensions above the fifth dimension, attaining this fifth level must be the first and immediate vibrational goal for the beings of Earth because this is where a quantum leap occurs. One can realize their infinite god power and ability beginning at this level.

As one moves vibrationally into the fifth dimension, an entirely new set of dimensional laws take effect and work in favor of the ascending being. Higher levels of information are available to consciousness at this point, everything becomes much easier to achieve, and things become much more wonderful. A being also acquires many new abilities in the fifth dimension that could be considered supernatural. The fifth dimension has been called heaven, nirvana, Shamballa, and Brahman. This heavenly dimension emanates only love, peace, abundance, health, freedom, and joy, which are the six pillars of ascension. These six attributes of the fifth dimension are the most desired by all humans. But, interestingly, not one of these most-desired things is tangible.

Pleiadian teaching about heaven.
Someone asked, "Am I going to fly away to heaven one beautiful morning when I die?"
Here is our simple answer to this question. "No."
Here is the explanation of this answer, "First of all, one cannot die. One's body can die; however, one is not a body but an eternal being that has no beginning or end. Furthermore, one's body doesn't have to die either if it is correctly cared for and body cells are regenerated. "
"Secondly, one won't fly away to heaven one glad morning because there is nowhere to fly to, and there is certainly no time to get there. There is only one time and one place, right here and right now, eternally. "Heaven is not up in the sky; if you think it is, the birds will get there before you do." It is not a place one goes to but a state of being.

This heaven is the fifth dimensional, gamma state of consciousness, which resonates between 40-100 hertz frequency. This bliss or ecstasy state of consciousness manifests outwardly as a beautiful and perfect world. Perceiving this world or reality provokes intense feelings of awe and majesty."

How do you get to this heaven? A great master teacher said, "This kingdom is inside of you and all around you, right now and right here, but you just can't see it yet." This master teacher illustrated that heaven is already here, on Earth, now, and everyone is standing in the midst of it. It's just that until one is resonating at its level, one cannot see it. One must be aligned vibrationally with this kingdom of heaven dimension to perceive it.

To get to this heaven, one must raise themselves to it. This raising of oneself is the daily mindful work of increasing one's vibrational level and is the divine ascension to heaven. The way to ascend to this divine realm is described in detail in our Ascension Chapter.

When the fifth primary DNA strand becomes active and connects to the fifth chakra portal, fifth-dimensional light flows through the body, and consciousness can decode that dimension. A new fifth-dimensional outer reality is then manifested by the consciousness decoding it, and the external world that exists right here and right now transforms into this heaven.

This heaven is in no single place but exists everywhere, even on Earth. Some call it the New Earth or The Fifth-dimensional Earth.

"Behold, I saw a new heaven and a new earth, for the old heaven and the old earth had passed away."

Heaven, the fifth dimension, is a glorious reality one can experience. It is ten thousand times greater than anything experienced in the third dimension. The implications are phenomenal here because one could be in this heaven by lunchtime tomorrow if they could elevate their internal vibration up just a few more notches. This notion provides a primary incentive to do the inner work necessary to expand consciousness levels.

Under the divine laws of free will and sovereignty, everyone is responsible for their journey to heaven. Though one has access to master spiritual guides and teachers along this journey, no one can do this work for another, and no other being can get you there.

One doesn't have to believe in dogma, rely on other divine beings, or even try and be good to go to heaven. They must open their energy centers, including the heart and throat chakras; then, one shall become love, truth, and light and dwell in this beautiful celestial kingdom. The master who has an evolved consciousness not only has access to this heavenly fifth-dimensional realm, but they are also the bringer of it to Earth.

Chapter 8: DNA

"The entire cosmos is written into the human body."
The Pleiadians

DNA is a biological quantum computer module that receives, stores, and transmits universal light. This light is a cosmic library that contains the templates and programmed instructions that create life itself. One can think of DNA as the universal language of all life.

If one contemplates this universal programming language, one must conclude that some very advanced being or group of beings devised and compiled this programming language.

There are twelve primary strands of DNA inside the human body. These primary DNA strands resonate with a corresponding chakra portal, and both resonate with a corresponding dimension and a state of consciousness.

The twelve primary DNA strands are present in the original divine and perfected twelfth-dimensional human genetic template. When an inactive primary DNA strand becomes activated, it joins a helix bundle with other active strands. The more strands bundled together in one's DNA helix, the higher their consciousness level is. Though many beings on Earth have three active strands of DNA in their helix, the most unconscious beings of the third dimension are not even in the third dimension. They are in the second dimension, and a double helix equates to a base survival level of consciousness. Many of the starseeds on Earth today currently possess a four-stranded DNA helix and the masters on Earth today possess at least five active bundled strands.

When a resonant frequency of light contacts a primary DNA strand, the strand is stimulated and receives this cosmic light into the body's cells. This process occurs in a quantum way outside the standard physics of time and space. Since DNA is not linear but multi-dimensional, it can directly access the quantum field and change matter. DNA has a function that works as a multi-dimensional induction antenna and receives this light information directly from the quantum field via a corresponding multidimensional chakra portal. The primary DNA strands of the human body were designed to attach electromagnetically to their corresponding and resonant chakra portals or ports. When a chakra port is open and spinning clockwise at light speed, universal light that resonates at that dimensional level then begins flowing into the chakra portal, the DNA strand is attached back to its resonant chakra, and the strand becomes activated or active. These activations usually occur in sequential order from the lower chakras up to the higher ones. As the life-force energy activates within DNA and moves up through the body's chakras, it is referred to as kundalini rising.

Since DNA also serves as the perfect light data storage device, the underlying informational field contained within the light is stored inside the DNA strand. The universal quantum field (light) contains massive amounts of information, but the original programmers thought this through, and it's certainly no issue for a DNA strand. Hard drives don't hold a candle to a DNA strand when storing information in general because the human genetic code can store billions of gigabytes in a single gram. Think of a DNA strand as a biological flash drive that allows the blueprints of life to be stored and passed between generations and species. Just like human cells, the crystals of Earth also receive and store huge amounts of this cosmic light and broadcast it outwardly across the entire planet for the beings of Earth to receive.

After a DNA strand becomes active, it transmits this light throughout the entire body via nadis which operate like tiny fiber optic cables, making the light information available to the consciousness that inhabits the body. DNA further transmits its stored light outwardly through its matching chakra portal, making it available for others to receive. You are becoming a master of receiving, storing and transmitting light. In fact, your primary mission for coming to Earth was to hold high-vibrational light in your body to raise the vibration of all humanity.

The magnificent beings spoken of in the bible, which came to Earth 450,000 years ago, used the original perfected, twelve-stranded DNA blueprint to create modern homo sapiens. These creators were master geneticists that did a bit of gene editing and spliced their genome with a primitive hominid of ancient Earth and came up with a brand-new species of human. To ensure their human creations were easy to control and that they would not be aware of what happened, these creators intentionally deactivated all but two of humanity's primary DNA strands. These inactive strands of DNA have been called junk DNA; however, these ten strands allow the highest levels of consciousness in this universe, and these strands hold the highest potential for humanity.

When these geneticists first created humans, they had to devise a way to make their genetics fit with Earth's hominid being. If one notices, chromosome two in the modern Earth human is not single: it is the splicing of two chromosomes, two-A and two-B, which were fused to form a composite chromosome two. Put differently; the second chromosome has another entire chromosome "tacked" onto it to carry twenty-four chromosomes in the space of twenty-three.

Since humanity was built from the perfected twelve-stranded DNA human template, humanity is indeed a divine creation with all its divinity intact. Moreover, humanity's creators left the dormant DNA strands inside the body, and every Earth human can reattach and re-activate these inactive strands.

Light is the primary modality for activating a primary DNA strand. Since humanity is moving up to the fifth-dimensional state of consciousness, the fifth primary DNA strand is activated by 40-100 hertz gamma light. Though high levels of this high-vibrational gamma light are now flowing into planet Earth from the galactic core, there must be a light receptacle to receive it. Furthermore, fifth-dimensional gamma light can only enter the nucleus of DNA through an open and spinning fifth chakra portal, the throat chakra.

The DNA activation process is ultimately about clearing and opening a chakra portal. Resonant light itself assists in opening a chakra portal; however, one must also do the inner work necessary to clear any energy blockages from a chakra. We discuss chakras in detail in Chapter 9. Another term that describes the DNA activation process is 'ascension.' Our Ascension Chapter details the various modalities for achieving DNA activation.

Approximately 4.5 billion starseeds live on Earth today; however, only about 20% have an activated fourth strand of primary DNA. Though the remaining other 80% feel they are very different from third-dimensional humanity, these starseeds have yet to fully awaken to who and what they truly are. The Pleiadians are here to provide triggers for these awakening starseeds so they will regain their ancient divine memories and begin to see the whole picture at just the right moment.

The great awakening is indeed underway on earth, and as humanity's frequency continues to rise, they will gain more access to higher consciousness. The dormant parts of the energy body are activating more than ever now, and new worlds and possibilities that were not available before are coming into view.

DNA is merging the physical body with the divine body, and the human being is well into its next phase of evolution.

Chapter 9: Chakras

Chakras are non-physical energetic connections that exist in all matter in the universe. Of course, a human body has chakra energy centers, but so does every other biological lifeform, every tree, rock, planet, star, and the cosmos itself has chakra energy centers.

A chakra is an energetic opening in the universe that functions as a multi-dimensional portal or stargate (aka/wormhole) for transporting universal light information. This light can instantly move through these portals across the universe in a quantum way outside the laws of time and space. All teachings in this book illustrate the importance of higher consciousness; however, if the universal light information that consciousness decodes as reality doesn't have a multidimensional way to flow into the human body, consciousness would always remain low. Furthermore, if there were no chakra portals, one could not shift across space and time or experience an NDE or out-of-body experience. The multi-dimensional chakra portal or simply 'multi-dimensional portal' is the only travel way through the universe.

Twelve primary chakra portals exist from the universal macro to the micro level. Each of the twelve chakra energy centers resonates within the specific frequency range and corresponds to one of the base-twelve dimensions of this universe, to one of the base-twelve levels of consciousness, and to one of the base-twelve primary DNA strands of the human body system.

There is only one set of twelve multidimensional chakra portals in this universe, and everything has this one set of twelve chakras in common. The same twelve chakra portals in the human body exist in any other object. One shares these same energy centers with all other beings, with all animals, with a mountain, with an ocean, and with the Earth itself.

Here are the names of these twelve chakra points concerning their location in the human body system. In the list below, The higher the number of the chakra, the higher its vibration and position are in the body or above it. The higher the resonance and position of a body chakra, the more light moves through it.

Chakra 1: Root Chakra
Chakra 2: Sacral Chakra
Chakra 3: Solar Plexus Chakra
Chakra 4: Heart Chakra
Chakra 5: Throat Chakra
Chakra 6: Third Eye Chakra
Chakra 7: Crown Chakra
Chakra 8: Soul Star Chakra
Chakra 9: Spirit Star Chakra
Chakra 10: Universal Chakra
Chakra 11: Galactic Chakra
Chakra 12: Divine Gateway Chakra

In the physical human body, a chakra energy center exists in the etheric layer, and a chakra energy center works hand in hand with a corresponding primary DNA strand. As we stated in our DNA chapter, a primary strand of DNA will only reattach electromagnetically to its corresponding chakra if the chakra is open and spinning, so light can flow through it.

These energetic portals or ports are integrated directly into one's being and their layered bodies, giving one a direct connection to the entire universe. There are seven chakras or energy centers in the physical body and five above the body. Even activating the eighth chakra, the star chakra just above the head, opens the doorway to incredible knowledge and supernatural abilities.

Each of the first seven chakras is located near a major body vessel organ and regulates a specific area of our being and life. As an energy worker, one knows these chakra energy centers can become blocked by low-vibrational energies, causing them not to function correctly. These lower-vibe energies are the traumas, dramas, and toxins picked up in life and stored in the energetic body. The electromagnetic energy of a healthy chakra energy center spins at light speed in a clockwise direction. In some cases, low vibe energies trapped in the body can cause a chakra energy center to stop spinning completely, greatly slow down, or even spin in the wrong direction. Since chakras govern different areas of life, this anti-energy manifests outwardly and will cause some issues. One must do the inner work necessary to transmute all lower vibrational energies stored in the body so the chakras are cleared and are spinning correctly. When a chakra energy center is not functioning optimally, one will experience a feeling of being stuck in the area of life the chakra governs. Since the material world of life is manifested by the light of the quantum field, if this light is not flowing through a chakra port, one would certainly be stuck. One will also experience health issues in the area of the body where the chakra center is located.

Since a chakra energy center produces a subtle spinning electromagnetic field, a master energy worker can detect malfunctioning chakras by performing a pendulum test. The energy worker can then help in unblocking the chakra.

Our Ascension Chapter discusses clearing any lower vibrational energies and toxins from the layered body system.

Let's look at chakra energy centers now on a larger scale regarding their physical locations on planet Earth.

The twelve primary chakras of Earth.
1.   Maui, Hawaii
2.   Lake Titicaca, Bolivia/Peru
3.   Tibet/India
4.   Yucatan Peninsula, Mexico
5.   Mt Shasta, California, USA
6.   Uluru, Australia
7.   Machu Picchu, Peru
8.   Glastonbury, England
9.   Giza Plateau
10.   Mount Cook, New Zealand
11.   Mt Ida /Hot Springs, Arkansas, USA
12.   Antarctica

These are the most energetic locations on the planet and where major ley lines of energy intersect. All these earth chakras feature magnificent ancient megalithic stone architecture or massive, underlying quartz crystal beds. The ancients intentionally placed these stone and crystal structures on these energetic spots to modulate the energy of that location for dimensional travel. All these Earth chakra points feature rock doorways that seem to lead nowhere or do nothing. Still, the ancients employed different methods to raise their frequency while standing in these portals using light, sound, and monatomic gold. They could transport themselves to higher dimensional realities via these stargates.

"All multidimensional travel occurs through one's chakras."
The Pleiadians

Think of an Earth chakra or stargate as a natural teleportation machine. The only reason one would use a machine to teleport instead of consciousness alone is that the machine creates an amplified electromagnetic field creating much more energy, making a reality shift easier.

Moving through an Earth stargate involves the process we discussed in our Space and Time Chapters for shifting into alternate realities. It's just that when one performs this reality-shifting process while inside the powerful electromagnetic energy vortex of one of these Earth chakras or portals, an incredible amount of extra 'teleporting' energy is made available. These Earth portals were designed to facilitate the conscious multidimensional travels of Earthly beings. Though aligned with specific star systems, these portals do not have fixed travel destinations in the stars that one shifts to. Instead, when one moves through an Earth portal, their destination of reality is solely chosen by intent and conscious vibration. While one can move through one of these Earth portals, they are also moving through their matching body chakra. A being that travels multidimensionally is ultimately moving through a portal in his own body via the merkaba. This stargate or chakra traveling is a very real trip to a very real, different reality; however, it is just not a physical trip; it's a shift of consciousness. Even on the cosmos' grand scale, these twelve primary energy portals or chakras exist throughout this universe. Any galactic civilization that seemingly travels across the vastness of space or dimensions is simply moving through one of these portals.

As the starseeds of Earth work hard to clear old, low-vibrational energies from their being, higher energy centers are opening, allowing more high-vibrational light to enter the body. As a result, many beings of Earth are opening their heart chakras for the first time, causing pure, divine love to flow. Others are working to open their fifth-dimensional throat chakra, where they will begin to speak and live their inner truth for the first time. When the fourth chakra opens, a being moves into the fourth-dimensional ascension school and is said to be well on their way to mastery.

When the fifth chakra opens, the fifth-dimensional light of the universe pours in, and a being becomes the master. At this point, one can

finally walk into a heaven on Earth that can be
seen.

Chapter 10: Ascension

"Your very purpose is to evolve your consciousness."
The Pleiadians

Approximately 350,000 years ago, advanced fifth-dimensional geneticists created Earth humanity. These first Earth humans were indigenous to this planet, and their descendants still walk the Earth today; however, another species came along later and began co-existing with native Earth humanity. This other species is just as human looking as native Earth humans; however, this other species does not originate from Earth. Instead, these other-worldly humans came from fifth-dimensional star systems to assist Earth humans in their conscious evolution. These benevolent star beings are referred to as Starseeds and are no less than angelic beings in human form.

"Humanity was created a little lower than the angels but are crowned with glory and honor."
The Pleiadians

Fifth-dimensional starseeds knew before they came to Earth that the best way to help raise the vibrational level of native Earth humans was to blend in as one of them and to provide this assistance from the inside out. Therefore, Starseeds agreed to lower their density and come into the lower physical realm, incarnated as the children of native Earth humans. Unfortunately, this coming down to Earth involved coming with a state of amnesia about the trip itself and about who and what one truly is. Furthermore, the starseeds agreed to begin their journey on Earth with none of their higher supernatural abilities intact.

Around 4.5 billion of these starseeds are walking on the Earth today; however, since they have lived closely among third-dimensional humans for so long, many assume that this is what they are. A

Starseed human is certainly no better than a native human; it's just that they typically have an additional primary strand of DNA active and operate at a higher level of consciousness. One's consciousness detects this species difference; therefore, young starseeds are often the black sheep of human families. They usually feel they don't fit in or that something must be wrong with them. In time, and as one evolves their consciousness, the truth behind this being different is revealed, and one then accepts and even begins to embrace who and what one truly is.

You are a divine being that came to Earth on a grand mission. You are here on Earth, helping humanity evolve its consciousness, and you are doing this process with them. As a part of the Earth collective, you are working to evolve your own being back to the higher realms where you started from.

This was the hardest mission ever undertaken in the universe, and you knew all that was involved before you came. Before you departed on your mission to Earth, you created a magnificent plan that included every detail of every lifetime on Earth. You planned the wonderful stuff that would happen to you, and you also planned the not-so-wonderful stuff. One may ask, "Why would I create hardship for myself this way?" We know the answer because we were there with you, helping you put your plan together. You did this because, in the state of perfection where you came from, there is no duality or contrast, and you desired to experience the duality and contrast of the third dimension and to see how you would overcome it. You considered what it would be like to come down from a perfected state, lowering your vibrational density. You were aware that lowering one's vibration equals pain and suffering. You considered the goodness of relieving the sufferings of others first, so after your contemplation, you made the brave sacrifice on behalf of all humanity and the cosmos itself.

You then closed your eyes, took a deep breath, and jumped with all the others! From heaven to Earth, you came down!

Here you are, standing strong, and you have overcome the entire world. You are closer than ever to your end goal, and we applaud your courage and all you have achieved.

You know well that this ascension work is the hardest work one can ever do. It takes much time on Earth, often lifetimes, and one must endure many heartbreaks and tears and learn many lessons as one moves up and grows up. This ascension work takes effort, practice, and determination, and one must be diligent every moment of every day.

One must be truly ready for ascension and dedicate themselves to it wholly to become a fifth-dimensional master and to further elevate themselves into the divine realms that exist beyond the fifth dimension. Know that the universe is dedicated to supporting a being who seeks to evolve their consciousness. The universe has unlimited resources to invest in one's spiritual evolution, and one can depend on its generous and powerful assistance.

"Ascension is a way of life and a way of being."
The Pleiadians

Whether you are just beginning or are well into your ascension journey, it is good to ask yourself, "Am I approaching the development of my soul in a serious and dedicated way and with great resolve?"

The awakening of humanity is known by several names, such as the ascension, the great awakening, the event, the evolution of consciousness, and planetary liberation, to name a few. These titles refer to the same thing, and for the sake of this writing, we will call this evolutionary process the ascension.

There is a collective human ascension occurring right now on planet Earth, and then there is one's personal ascension occurring simultaneously. The focus must be on one's personal ascension as the collective ascension will take care of itself and occur naturally as each one works to raise their vibration and consciousness level. Positive change in the world begins with a positive change in one's personal life.

When we say ascension, we do not mean rising in the air physically or going to some physical place but experiencing a speeding up of one's sub-atomic vibration, which allows higher consciousness levels.

The phrase ascending to a higher realm or higher dimension is also a bit misleading as differently perceived realms are neither higher nor lower but are all in one place, right here. One shall perceive other dimensional realms outwardly but does not go to them; one shifts into these realms right here.

The twelve chapters of this book all discuss an important part of the ascension process. Everything discussed in this writing is interconnected, and each precept builds on the one before. All the information we presented up to this point forms the necessary foundational background for the ascension process.

Now it's time to do the work and if you are ready, let's finish this ascension together.

"Always vibrate high!"
The Pleiadians

To ascend to faster-vibrating dimensions and be able to perceive and experience their wondrous realities, one must engage in certain practices that will increase the vibration of their being. Nothing is more important than raising one's vibes because one can absolutely reach amazing levels of perfection, and ultimately, this perfection has no end.

Here are the primary ascension techniques for speeding up one's internal vibration.

The thing that affects one's vibration the most is the food they are eating, and the first and most powerful way to raise one's vibrational level is to only ingest high-vibrational energy foods.

One becomes what one eats, so ingesting high-vibrational food daily is required for light body development and ascension.

The golden rule is always to eat natural energy foods, known as superfoods. Superfoods contain the highest vibrational energy of all foods and promote optimal cellular function in the human body. Superfoods instantly begin nourishing the cells correctly, producing much more energy in the layered human body system.

"Eat light, and you shall become light."
The Pleiadians

Take the light energy of this naturally energetic food into your cells, and in time you will transform into this light. When one's vibrational frequency increases, the body's cells morph into soft crystals, and one must only feed them light, energetic substances to develop them.

Ingesting natural energy foods is not only critical for expanding consciousness but also for realizing instant health benefits. Chronic disease and illnesses in the human body system can be defined by having a low cell voltage, aka PH Level. Every cell in the body is programmed to run on -20 to -25 millivolts. Furthermore, to heal and regenerate, the body must create new cells, which requires -50 millivolts. Therefore, chronic disease occurs when cell voltage drops below -20 and/or one cannot achieve -50 millivolts to make new cells. The atomic energy contained in Superfoods dramatically increases cellular voltage after only hours of ingesting them. One will quickly notice the increase in energy and how much better one feels as all body systems move back into optimal levels of functionality and health.

"Eat only from Mother Gaia's table each day."
The Pleiadians

In the modern third-dimensional world, everything is convenient, and food is no exception. Most food in modern grocery stores is processed and has very little or no energetic value. To preserve this food and make it taste like food, much of it is altered genetically, and chemicals are added that can be detrimental to the human body's cells. Moreover, much of this food's healthy, nutritional part has been removed. These synthetic and modified food forms lower one's internal vibration and adversely affect health.

An alternative to conveniently relying on processed food is to obtain more healthy and pure food at a natural and organic food store.

Another more radical alternative is to grow one's own natural energy food. This requires an adequate tract of land, basic cultivation equipment, and knowledge of cultivation. However, growing one's own natural food is much healthier, and in the long run, it is less costly. Also, consider that this approach was not radical only a few decades ago and was the norm for everyone to provide food for themselves and their families. Providing one's own food supply is a major step towards becoming sovereign and self-reliant. If one becomes a master of cultivating, preparing, and ingesting natural energy foods, one will certainly realize how magnificent the food tastes. The combinations of incredible textures and flavors of this natural energy food are endless.

Water and food are the basic human survival requirements, so the same golden rule for food also goes for water. Always drink pure, natural water rich in magnesium, potassium, calcium, sodium, and other trace minerals. The primary struggle in the creation of the first Earth human was to figure out what kind of minerals promoted human life, and the creators discovered that the same minerals contained in the 'clay' of the soil of earth were what Earth beings were made of. Therefore, these minerals are a basic requirement for human life to develop.

Healthy eating is an area of ascension that takes determination and resolve, and if one is new to this way of eating, it can take some getting used to.

The first and best gift one can give to themselves to experience a fast and powerful boost of consciousness is to begin today ingesting only natural, energetic, whole superfoods. This powerful spiritual guidance will ensure a profound expansion of consciousness right away and is the best everyday health and improvement guidance that can be given to anyone.

Basic self-care and self-respect are key tenants of ascension, and these demand that eating healthy natural energy foods should be life priority number one.

It will be your task to research and create your list of the most healthy, energetic natural superfoods. It will also be your choice to decide what you will include and not include on this list and how to prepare this food. The last task is to decide where and how to obtain the superfood on your list.

"The only healing is natural healing."
The Pleiadians

The second most powerful way to raise one's cellular vibration and increase consciousness levels is to be in nature. If you notice, you will see that everything powerful, good and healthy comes from nature. This is because nature emanates the field and essence of life itself. Knowing this is the knowledge of the master.

The golden rule here is to spend as much time as possible immersed in nature.

The energy of nature is the very energy of the universe itself. This energy vibrates very high, and as one interacts with nature, their vibrational level is greatly increased.

As we illustrated above, with natural food, the vibrational qualities of nature heal and regenerate the human body. The layered human body system is an amazing creation with a built-in perfected healing program. This body is designed to heal itself naturally and automatically. Suppose this internal healing program is interrupted by low-vibrational energies and is not functioning optimally. In that case, one can allow the powerful healing energies of nature to help heal the body. Nature emits a universal harmonic pattern of perfection that will align the layered human body to its optimized state. All one must do to experience nature's healing effect is to be within its energetic field.

The Gospel of Peace.
Some beings came to the bank of the river and asked the master, "How can we be healed, for we are the most ill people on Earth?
The master said, "One cannot know the father until one first knows the mother."
"Who is the mother?" they asked.
The master said, "The mother is Gaia, the natural healing Earth, which sustains your very being."
Then the master said, "One cannot know the mother until one knows her angels."
"Who are these angels of the mother?" they asked.
And he said to them, "The angels of the Earth are four in number. The angels of the sun, the air, the water, and the angel of the ground."
Then they asked him, "But how can these angels heal us, master"?
He said, "Only come into their presence and remain there for seven days. Spend seven days

with the angel of the sun, seven days with the angel of the air, seven days with the angel of the water, and seven days with the angel of the clay; then you shall be healed."

Each one spent this time in nature, seven days each, with the angels of the Earth, and all of them were completely healed.

Nature is a divine, energetic organism that transfers great power into one's body, mind, and soul, and all one must do is make a connection to it.

Earth's sun is one of nature's most powerful energies, and the ancients taught that it was the source of life itself. One of the most powerful Pleiadian ascension rituals one can perform to expand conscious levels is solar yoga. In ancient times, solar yoga was called Vedic yoga, Vedic dharma, the yoga of the sun, and was referred to as the yoga of light by the ancient Lemurians. Ancient solar yoga is when one receives intelligent cosmic information through the human eye via direct solar gazing.

The ancient Vedas say the most powerful spiritual force in the universe is contained within the sun's rays. Solar yoga masters call this universal energy x-factor. X-factor is the ambrosia of ascension and conscious evolution and is the rocket fuel that will quickly power one's light-body ship toward home. The activation of x-factor causes a great change within the body. One of the main functions of x-factor is activating the primary life force centers within the human body. As the energy of x-factor is increased by solar yoga, the dormant energy of the life force centers is released.

"The light of the body is the eye."
The Pleiadians

The human eye is a miniature sun, and like the suns of the solar system, it can absorb and radiate light. It absorbs x-factor energy through the retina, from where it is redistributed to the brain and nervous system. The eye is the only exposed nerve in the human body. When it is directly connected to the Earth's sun via solar yoga, the optic nerve takes in large amounts of this universal x-factor which immediately stimulates higher DNA strands.

Experienced practitioners of solar yoga often combine other ascension methods and tools, including meditation, movement, mantras, nature, and crystals, with solar yoga. After ten minutes of direct solar yoga, one will experience an immediate activation and experience an expanded state of consciousness, finding themselves in a higher dimension, right where they are.

Learn from the masters on the correct procedure for receiving solar information through the eye.

The third-dimensional, modern matrix world has crowded in on nature, with concrete and steel structures, the generation of strong electrical and unhealthy EMF fields, and the emission of many harmful toxins. The energy emitted from this artificial matrix system is very dense and low and is not beneficial to sentient life. If one also notices, there is usually asphalt or concrete under their feet, and they are most likely wearing rubber-soled shoes, insulating their bodies from the beneficial energy of nature. However, if one looks beyond the artificial matrix of this world and looks just over there, one will notice that nature is not far away. They may see some trees and grass. They may see some rocks, hills or mountains, reservoirs of natural water, and even the ocean. If they raise their eyes and look up, they will most likely see the sky, the sun, and the moon.

One must intently decide to spend more time being closer to this nature each day to develop higher levels of consciousness and create optimal health. Moreover, one's existence in the physical realm ultimately depends on it, and in the beginning, humanity itself was created to exist in the life-sustaining paradise of nature.

Please make time to experience nature's divine beauty and take it all in, using every physical sense. Become intimate with nature and its powerful energies, and you will ascend!

"The universe is mind, and meditation is the tool used to operate it."
The Pleiadians

Deep transcendental meditation is a primary and powerful way to raise one's internal vibration, greatly expanding one's consciousness levels. Meditation also produces profound, tangible healing results. For example, many master meditators can heal diseased or damaged body parts in minutes, not only in their own bodies but in others' bodies.

Furthermore, transcendental meditation can completely reprogram the subconscious mind and allow the rapid physical manifestation of anything one can imagine. Chapter 12 discusses the special states of consciousness attained during meditation that allow direct access to the subconscious mind. The subconscious mind controls nearly all physical life and is the source of all physical manifestations. Practice visualizing and focusing on your desires while meditating to improve manifestation skills greatly.

When one becomes a master of entering deep states of meditation, one can contact the source of all that is. It has been said that a great kingdom exists inside one's being, and if God is sitting on the throne inside the temple of heaven, one must go inside the temple to commune with this God. The human body is the temple of God and is where God dwells. Going inward into deep meditative states is to enter this grand temple, where contact occurs. This God being has been called by many names, including the higher self and source energy. It is a profound experience when one connects to this internal energy source. Many have described feeling intense emotions of awe, expansion, and complete oneness when this occurs. While this experience is quite amazing, there is a higher level of it that is truly mind-boggling. To meet this great being in person is one thing, but fully realizing its true identity is another. As one meditates deeper and keeps reaching higher on their spiritual ascension journey, one inevitably comes to the awareness that this grand God being that is the source of all things is, ultimately, themselves. When this profound truth is experienced, with it comes the realization of one's incredible and unlimited creative power. In this knowing, the master becomes humble and responsible in every way and begins to live and operate from this powerful inner knowing.

Meditation is an effective way to open the twelve chakra portals and reactivate all twelve primary DNA strands. All twelve levels of consciousness can be attained through meditation. As discussed in our Space and Time Chapters, meditation is the modality used to explore and shift to all space-time realities of the universe.

Meditation is a requirement for accessing higher levels of consciousness, and one must spend time first learning about, then practicing, all aspects of it to become a master meditator. When one attains this mastery, they will see that they have not only taken control of all lower laws but also taken control of the entire universe.

Sacred breathwork is the lead-up to deep meditations. Breathing in and out slowly and deeply changes one's brainwaves or vibrational rate, which is the induction into different meditative states of consciousness.

This slow and deep breathwork is also one of the fastest mind and body healing techniques known. Sacred breathwork is the prana of life that aligns and repairs all body systems in minutes.

If anxiety becomes present, one can practice mindful, conscious breathwork to quickly bring the body back to its calm, natural state.

A powerful electromagnetic toroidal vortex is produced by sacred breathwork called 'prana' that works in a quantum way to change matter. This energetic field is emitted several feet from the human body and, when mixed with conscious intention, can instantly alter the outer physical world. Think of breathwork as a powerful, divine ability to control and change the reality around you in seconds and minutes. With every deep and slow breath, one's being is elevated into higher and higher levels of consciousness that alter the outer realm. If you desire or need to change something outwardly, breathe the change in and out deeply and slowly, then watch the magic happen.

Crystals are incredible metaphysical tools one can use on their journey of ascension. The crystals of Earth are beautiful and structured geometric creations of nature that can control vibrational energy, providing benefits for elevating one's consciousness level.

All crystals on Earth were originally brought down from fifth-dimensional star systems billions of years ago by ancient builder races and seeded on this planet. The beings that brought these crystals to Earth knew they were organic living entities that must be planted, cultivated, and grown just like the seeds of a garden. Think of the term 'crystal bed,' which sounds much like a bed of plants, and notice that rough forms of quartz, such as amethyst and citrine, have roots on their end, just like a plant. Ancient writings in the care of the Atla Ra Priesthood that still exist today from Atlantean times say the great crystal beds of Brazil and Arkansas, USA, were seeded in these locations by the Atlanteans. They cultivated these magnificent crystal beds to produce large, colorful, translucent master crystals for their temples and cities worldwide. This ancient priesthood describes the magnificent pieces of colorful quartz produced in modern-day Arkansas as 50 cubits in length and weighing several hundred tons. They describe these otherworldly pieces as an amalgam of quartz, pure gold, silver, and platinum. Twelve of these sublime and magnificent master crystals were placed around the main island of Atlantis, and each crystal emitted a different color of light that lit up the cities and could be seen for miles.

The ancient civilizations of Earth fully understood the properties of crystal technology, and these advanced races used crystals to power and operate nearly every aspect of their society. Many high-conscious starseeds on Earth today have a strong, energetic attraction to crystals. During incarnations in ancient times, you had an intimate relationship with crystals and worked with them each day in the magnificent temples of healing and rejuvenation.

Modern science on Earth is yet to realize the secret inner workings and power of crystals, primarily because they only attempt to understand them from a physical point of view.

The great masters know that to gain the power of the crystal, one must approach them in a non-linear way, and as Nikola Tesla said, "One must think in terms of energy, frequency, and vibration."

"A crystal itself is energetically neutral, and crystals alone do not do anything; however, when any form of energy is presented to a crystal, it then performs a specific function on the energy introduced."
The Pleiadians

Crystals work as multi-functional energy controllers, and crystals do this work on a quantum and multi-dimensional level.

The ancients used crystals to convert all forms of energy into other forms for powering their advanced, technical civilizations. They also performed metaphysical feats using crystal technology that would seem like magic today.

Though crystals can modulate all forms of energy, the primary energy we are speaking of, concerning ascension, is the energy of the quantum field, the energy of the universe, aka, the electromagnetic field of light. Photons carry tiny packets of information over large distances and are entangled in relatively large numbers. Think of the sun's light or the even higher-vibrational light emitted by the cosmos when it makes contact with a crystal.

Crystals function like modern semiconductors and can receive, conduct, transmit, store, amplify, switch, transduce, resist, oscillate, and even transform light into other forms of energy. The specific function that will be executed on the light energy that enters a crystal, like a superconductor, depends on the crystal's lattice structure.

One of the signature properties of a crystal or gemstone is its refractive index. We will focus on a primary type of refraction here: isotropic, cubic, single-light refractive. Photons move through the internal lattice of atoms of a single light refractive crystal at a constant angle in all directions at the same speed. Therefore, single-light refractive crystals are the most powerful for energy management and ascension. These single-light refractive crystals include diamonds, garnets, and spinel. These crystals naturally receive, amplify and refract powerful beams of high vibrational light into the body's auric field by default. Furthermore, the colorful rainbow auras emitted when these crystals are exposed to light is the equivalent of modern LED light therapy developed by NASA.

Quartz crystal is another very important ascension tool. When quartz crystals are subject to photonic light fields, they start the generation of scalar energy. Scalar energy is when the third-dimensional waveform is canceled out and removed by an opposing waveform, and only the higher vibrational part of the wave remains. Using light as an example, we can see how light bounces back and forth in the facets as it moves through a crystal. Because the light is being refracted, a certain percentage of the light will go out of phase to the original beam and cancel itself out. This is where the scalar or zero-point energy is generated. This scalar energy can pass through an object in 3D because it travels in a higher dimension. When one transduces this scalar information into a lower-dimensional object, that object then takes on part of the scalar transmission and becomes transmuted. Furthermore, the scalar energy produced by a quartz crystal is stored in its crystal matrix, amplified, and transmitted back out for another to receive. This entire process works in a quantum way regardless of time and space.

The energetic functions of high-frequency, clear quartz crystals are further increased when the crystals are cut or faceted, on the outside, in a certain way. The ancients knew this and used to cut particular facets using sacred geometry on their crystals to increase power output and achieve a focused beam of energy. When a quartz crystal is cut this way, the refractive properties enhance the generation of the scalar waveform. Cutting geometric PHI and golden mean shapes on the outside of the crystal creates a natural mirror effect that enhances the inside's scalar light reflections.

Now let's go a step further. What happens in a non-linear way when conscious thoughts and intentions are sent into the crystal? The thought or intention energy is mixed with the existing scalar energy, transmuted into its highest form, and stored in the crystal matrix. The crystal lattice then performs its internal semiconductor functions on the new energy by amplifying and transmitting the new energy outwardly as the newly manifested reality.

Crystals are powerful natural ascension tools that modulate etheric energy in different ways to benefit the body's auric field. Know crystals' different structures and superconductive properties to gain their energetic benefit. Keep your favorites near the body's electromagnetic field and greatly enhance your life force.

Sound is another powerful ascension tool that can directly increase consciousness levels. As discussed in our Sound Chapter, sound is a primary creative force of consciousness that can be used in different ascension modalities, including music, singing, mantras, chants, power words, positive affirmations, toning, and binaural beats. Surround your being with the magical harmonies of the universe and fill yourself with the sound of the spheres to be lifted to divine realms.

Forms of art, energetic movement, and creativity are also powerful ways to raise one's vibration. As a divine creator, one is most aligned and fulfilled when creating. This is because, as a universal creator, this is your primary nature.
Fill your life with beautiful colorful art and magical creations. Move with the universe's flow by

dancing and practicing yoga daily. Study sacred geometry to see how it is the creation template and use its mathematical beauty in your divine creations.

The Pleiadians teach that light is information and darkness lacks information. Therefore, to have light, and be the light, spend time each day gaining sacred knowledge on many subjects. With the advent of the modern Internet, much knowledge is available; one just has to seek it earnestly. Question everything you study and especially question everything you think you know. Ask yourself who taught you about the primary subjects of life. Seek more knowledge about a subject to see if there is more to the story; there always is. Take a fresh look at different subjects from a more expanded and higher viewpoint. Dig deeper into things because the more information one has, the more light one has. The more light one has, the more expanded their conscious awareness is, and the more ability and power one has.

Sometimes it's best to take an entire belief system that seems contradictory or errant and chuck it into the trash bin. After you chuck it, however, start building a new belief system about that subject based on one precept of truth at a time. This way, one will arrive much closer to the highest truth. Do not necessarily believe every conspiracy theory or myth but realize there is most likely a core of truth in each one.

Belief systems are useful along one's ascension journey; however, know that any belief system itself is a limiting box placed around a thing that doesn't allow for the other endless possibilities a thing may be. We live in an unlimited universe filled with unlimited quantum possibilities of all that is. As one gains high levels of knowledge in many areas, one tends to merge most belief systems into an overall way of thinking that is more like a theory of everything.

As you move along your evolutionary path, we suggest diving into metaphysics, different sciences, ancient history, prehistory, and conscious expansion. These areas of deep study will fill one's being with pure light as one takes it all in. Read the ancient books and manuscripts, study the ancient stone tablets, listen to the master teachers on audio and watch their teachings on video. Turning off the matrix political and crime news along with low-vibe drama and trauma television shows is important. Instead, switch to daily higher-consciousness media. Doing this alone will greatly expand consciousness and improve everything in one's life.

Most importantly, have fun with it all!

"Have fun all the time!"
The Pleiadians

Let's face it; if something isn't fun for someone, then one's vibration is low. In everything we have suggested in this chapter, it is critical to approach it all like a small child and have the ultimate fun with it. If it's not fun, see why not and start making it fun. Laugh and play in whatever you do daily, and have fun. We can't think of anything greater to tell you than these words. Do only what you love and enjoy every now moment of life. Live life to the fullest because this is the whole purpose of living. When you do things you enjoy and things that make you feel good, you speed up every particle in your cells and make them spin faster than the speed of light!

The Pleiadians

We've saved the most important part of ascension and the best part of this chapter for last. Let's talk about love.

The primary emotional characteristic of the intelligence behind the universe is love. Love is the essence of creative source energy, and love is the great power of the intelligence that creates all things.

You have heard that God is love. It is also said that this love is patient and kind. It does not envy; it does not boast; it is not proud. It is not rude, it is not self-seeking, it is not easily angered, and it keeps no record of wrongs. This love does not delight in evil but rejoices in goodness and truth. It always protects, always trusts, hopes, and always perseveres. Therefore, one can always count on this love. One can place all their trust and faith in it because this love never fails.

The essence and identity of the highest being in this universe is unconditional love. As discussed throughout this book, this great divine being is you!

Here is the Pleiadian teaching about God and love. The teaching has two parts.

The first part of the teaching says, "Love yourself with all your heart, mind, and soul."

Before we go further, the one who understands this teaching knows very well that self-love is in no way about an ego, narcissism, or being selfish in any way, which is all, in fact, the opposite of love.

Many have believed that true love is always putting others first and themselves last. A higher conscious being realizes they cannot give something to another that they do not possess. Furthermore, universal law says one cannot manifest (receive) a thing that one has not first given to themself. This immutable law holds true for all things, including love. One cannot receive love from another person unless they have given themselves the same level of love. Also, one can only be of significant energetic assistance or service to any other after they have enough personal energy stored to be of any quality service. One will indeed be in great service to all humanity, but only after they have first filled themselves with the great power of love.

The second part of this teaching says, "Love all others, the same as yourself, with all of your heart, mind, and soul." To fulfill both parts of this divine instruction is to fulfill all universal law.

A major step of the ascension journey is to show yourself the highest levels of love and healthy self-respect. This step is critical for making significant progress in one's ascension.

"Gift to yourself first."
The Pleiadians

The first step on the journey to self-love is to give yourself some nice things and to do some nice things for yourself. You do this the same way you would for a dear loved one, except you're doing it for yourself. Take yourself to your favorite place and do some things you would like to do. Take yourself shopping and buy some nice clothes or things you want. Make a list of wonderful things you can give to yourself and start giving! When you do this, you will begin receiving awesome things in all areas of life. This is the beginning of love; it is an incredible feeling, and it is a high vibration!

"One can only receive what they give."
The Pleiadians

Immutable universal law dictates that everyone always gets only and exactly what they give, all the time, every time. One may say, "Well, that evil person did not receive what they gave." We tell you that even the one who did evil, by law, must receive the exact thing they gave out energetically. The exact moment when this receiving will occur is the domain of the universe, but be assured, it will occur, and the universe is perfectly fair and just.

The universe always gives one an equal measure of what they have given, regardless if it is given to others or themselves. Remember, others and self are ultimately the same, and there is really only one of us here.

The love you give to yourself, you possess. What you possess, you can then give to another. Both forms of giving love are then returned in equal measure by the universe and further given to you.

Another gift of love you can give to yourself is to set up some new safe energy boundaries. Giving yourself this gift is critical because you won't progress too far along your new ascension plan if you do not complete this step early on. While one is working to elevate their vibrational level to the fifth dimension, one must love themselves enough to keep all low-vibrational energies at a safe distance because these toxic energies drastically lower one's vibration and consciousness levels. After one becomes a fifth-dimensional master, their high vibration becomes dominant and either repels or transmutes all lower energies; however, until one reaches that point, one must create energetic barriers to block out these lower energies. These lower, draining energies include toxic people and relationships, environmental toxins, and third-dimensional matrix toxins. The specifics on how to correctly block these lower energies by creating energetic boundaries are discussed in our Sovereignty Chapter.

On the journey to love and ascension, one must not only raise their vibrational level but also do the necessary inner work to clear any old, low-vibrational energy from their being.

Since energy can never be destroyed but only transmuted, as a survival mechanism, energies emitted from traumatic events that are too much for the conscious mind to process are stored in the subconscious mind.

These lower energies are stored there, so they can be dealt with later when one's consciousness has developed enough to transmute them. But, of course, everyone has to deal with even the tiniest of traumas eventually. Still, in many cases, a being can carry this negative stored energy inside for a lifetime or even multiple lifetimes until they can finally process it. The problem with keeping this energy swept under the rug, and out of the way, even for a few days, weeks or months, is that an unpleasant thing that matches this energy must manifest. Furthermore, it will stay manifested in one's life until its underlying energy is cleared.

All mental energy, especially subconscious energy, manifests outwardly into the physical world. This low-vibe energy manifests itself first as physical body ailments near the area of the body that was most affected by the trauma. This area of the body is always near one of the major organs and one of the body's energy chakras. Both the organ and the chakra are affected adversely by this energy. Since the body's chakras control all aspects of one's physical world, the stored low-vibrational trauma energy will manifest outwardly as problems in the area of life the chakra controls. Another serious issue is that since this energy is hidden in and manifested by the unconscious, one's moods, behaviors, feelings, and responses to life will all be affected adversely without the conscious mind even knowing this is happening.

To transmute these lower energies from one's being, one must first bring the energy up from the subconscious mind to the conscious mind. This is done by reaching the alpha state of consciousness during meditation and by doing some deep inner reflection at the same time into why a negative thing keeps manifesting itself, in cycles, in an area of one's life.

Light is information, and darkness is the lack of information. As the light of alpha conscious observance shines on something hidden in the unconscious mind, the hidden thing will eventually show itself. Observe it and allow it to be what it is when the energy comes up.

Sit with it long enough to gain its information. This energy simply has needed to express itself, and after it does, it has no other purpose. View this energy as a shadow of an unreal past and see that it has no reality in your current moment. After doing this healing meditation, one then has more information, and this new information leads to seeing a thing as it truly is and to a state of acceptance and letting go. This acceptance and letting go is the energetic transmutation process. This energetic transmutation corrects the health issues occurring around the body's organ. It also frees up the spin of the affected chakra allowing its corresponding level of light to begin pouring into the chakra.

If more than one traumatic event has occurred in one's life, do the above exercise with each one. It takes resolve, inner strength, and courage to do this work, but it is one of the greatest gifts one can give to themselves and is certainly the most liberating spiritual work one can do.

Chapter 11: Sovereignty

As we discussed in Chapter 1, the greatest level of enlightenment is to realize who and what one truly is and to start being this. You are the very essence and consciousness of the universe dwelling in a human body, as you. Therefore, we could say your true identity is God expressing itself as you. Remember, consciousness is singular, and this same identity applies to all beings, and there is no being that is not this.

You are the highest being in all existence, and no other being is above you. Therefore, you are completely sovereign, and no one has authority over you.

Before one can be truly sovereign, one must be aware of the caveats of this divine way of being. While societies may have tens of thousands of laws to follow, there is only one law for the sovereign to follow. The Pleiadians call this one law the great instruction. This great law is the law of love. This love does no harm and fulfills all other laws. When one adheres to this one universal law, they will be respecting and abiding by the rules of their collective society by default.

Human law systems often say something is someone else's fault, so blame is the name of the game on Earth. The Pleiadians do not use the concept of fault or blame but instead, use the term 'responsibility.' Both universal law and sovereignty are based on the divine concept of real responsibility, and as consciousness levels and heart levels expand, this becomes one's primary way of being.

One caveat of being sovereign is that while no other has authority over you, you also do not have authority over any other. This is the law of free will, and since this universe is based on free will, free will must always be honored.

Some may think that sovereignty is about authority, control, and power, but it is more about energy and, specifically, human energy. It is said in Pleiadian sciences that a human being has more power inside than all the stars in the universe combined. This is the powerful energy we are speaking of and the most desired power in the universe.

It is important to understand that while this is a free-will universe, it is also a contractual universe where all things occur by contracts and agreements. These contracts are backed by real universal power that binds one to the contract. Since you are the highest being in the universe, built-in universal law says no other being can manipulate or control you without your permission. On the other hand, one being, or group of beings, can gain full authority and control over others if contractual permission for this is granted.

First of all, know that only a low-vibrational, unconscious being that is unhealthy energetically would be narcissistic and selfish enough to try to manipulate or control another being. These types of beings exist physically and non-physically, and since they have such a low amount of energy and power, they constantly work to steal energy from other beings. This energy we are speaking of is the vital life force that flows between all beings via energetic connections called energy cords.

Even these low vibrational energy stealers must abide by the universal law of contractual agreement and gain permission to use someone's life force. Even stranger sounding is that this permission has to be given by the one who is about to have their energy manipulated!

Why would someone give their permission to have their energy manipulated and used this way, and how is this contractual permission granted?

The first and most obvious way to grant consent for another to use one's energy is simply by being connected to them. Just forming an energetic connection equates to agreeing to the energetic connection, and this agreement is a binding universal contract. This 'being connected' takes on many forms. For example, an energetic cord is connected when one resonates vibrationally with another by being in the same space at the same time with them, by thinking about or focusing on them, and lastly, by being emotionally attached to them or something close to them. These energetic cords operate in a quantum way outside of space-time, so any perceived distance or time between two connected beings is irrelevant.

Regarding physical attachments, be aware that any heirloom or physical object carries energy from its past owner, and it is wise to know what this energy is. If one is not certain, the physical object should be removed from one's space, and any energetic attachment to it must also be removed. Often, these heirlooms are passed down through family lines or given as gifts and may have a high emotional or monetary value attached to them. However, the only true value these have is their energetic value, so regardless, it's wise to take inventory of all relics stored or lying around and to know the energy and intent behind them.

Stored phone numbers, texts, chats, messages, pictures, videos, music, etc., also carry the energy of other beings, their connections to others, and so on. This is a bit to keep up with, but one must keep themselves energetically clear of unhealthy, energetic cords. All data stored on mobile devices, social media connections, friends, and files stored, accessed, or transmitted on a computer amplify energetic connections because of the electronic circuitry and exponentially make the energy manipulation from others even more powerful. Unhealed low-vibrational beings often send electronic messages that would normally provoke a negative emotional reaction, and unfortunately, close, unhealed family members or so-called loved ones can be the worst for sending these messages to an ascending family member. The longer these types of messages are, the more negative they are and the more energy they drain off. These messages can sometimes be a bit threatening, usually stating that the ascending being has 'lost their mind' and they must return to normal at once or suffer consequences. If a newly ascending being receives a low-vibrational message like this, the first inclination is to be shocked, fearful, and hurt.

"The ascending being then may ask themselves, "How can the one who sent this message be so cruel?" In the early stages of ascension, one may retaliate from negative emotions and send a counter-message in defense. The negative energy is then amplified exponentially, but worse, vital life-force energy begins flowing from the ascending being into the other via an energetic cord. This energetic drain is experienced as the lowest possible emotional vibrations, and the physical body begins unmanifesting and deteriorating rapidly.
Have no fear because the sovereign is here!

The fifth-dimensional master of sovereignty can deal with this situation quickly if it arises and is not affected by it energetically.
First, the master of sovereignty knows that lower vibrational beings are not yet healed energetically, so their nature is to not always operate from true love, not to allow free will, and not to always want what is best for others, including their so-called

loved ones. These low-vibrational unhealed beings steal energy by default.

Secondly, the master of sovereignty does not place blame because it is understood that unhealed lower vibrational beings have no idea what's really happening here beyond noticing they feel re-vitalized after a negative reaction is achieved by their intimidating message. What's more, these low-vibers also have no awareness that they are themselves, being used as pawns by other low-vibrational beings in a vast energetic network created to drain human energy.

Third, the master of sovereignty knows that low-vibrational beings usually do not like seeing others moving away from the third-dimensional 'norm' or doing better than them. This is because every being is a reflective, energetic mirror for all others, and when third-dimensional humans see another doing well or changing even in a positive way, they are forced to look at themselves and see that maybe they're not doing so well in comparison. At this point, they often attack using various strategies to try and bring the ascending being back down to their level energetically. It's easier and safer for them to attack from a distance, and a modern electronic message is a perfect medium. Fourth, the master of sovereignty knows that connecting and communicating this way sparks an energetic war, and one's life force is the primary spoil of this war. Therefore, one golden rule is not to open or read these messages. Another important rule is always to remain silent. In this energetic war of words, the one who speaks first loses.

Above all, the sovereign master knows that the primary rule is not to be connected in the first place to beings who resonate this way. So if necessary, set up safe, energetic barriers, block the connections, and cut all the cords! This immediately removes contractual consent by connection for energetic manipulation. Afterward, change focus, don't give that connection another thought, and move on. This is your sovereign right. Before you move on, just make sure you delete the files, the messages, and the numbers, or the energy will still flow off of them.

Ascension and sovereignty require fortitude and wisdom but remember, at any point, any low-vibrational being can transmute their manipulating energies into pure unconditional love; however, this evolutionary process usually takes multiple lifetimes to achieve. The masters teach that in practical everyday terms, the odds of this 'transmutation or transformation to love process' occurring this year or even in this incarnation are very slim. People don't change this profoundly or this quickly as a rule, and this fact is just something to come to terms with.

One adult Starseed said, "My own mother is doing this to me!" "Don't I have to allow her controlling behavior because she is my mother?"

We say, "Honor your mother and father; however, they must honor you similarly." One must not allow themselves to be intimidated into any consensual contract under any form of low-vibrational guilt, fear, or illusionary obligation. The important work for you is to keep your focus on yourself, and it is always irrelevant what another is doing. Before we close this topic, keep in mind that if another is not fully encouraging and supporting your free will to be whatever you desire, regardless of their relationship to you, do they really love you to begin with? You know the answer, so think about it for a moment, then be true to yourself and act accordingly.

There is a high probability that someone close to you did not like the idea when you decided to improve your life (ascend). Furthermore, they did not like it so much that they decided to threaten you with war if you proceeded! All we desire for you here is to stop and think deeper about what happened and seek the truth of it. Then, when you see the truth of it, allow it to sink in. If a manipulative situation like this is currently happening in your life, we say, "Be true to yourself and hold your ground!" If you do this, the universe will quickly take care of the situation, surprisingly!

Another primary way 'consent to be manipulated' is granted is simply by being unaware it is happening. The unconscious and unaware one is easily led away, enslaved, and others can use their personal energy easily without their knowledge. The universe is just and allows this to occur because all parties have agreed for it to occur. Consent was granted, the contract was placed into force, and unconsciousness is not considered a valid defense in the great court of the universe. This is just how it works; as a sovereign being, it is fully one's responsibility to be conscious and to protect and manage their energy wisely.

A similar way to grant consent to have one's energy taken is to be tricked or deceived. Again, the universe requires one to be aware enough of what is happening around them not to allow this to occur before sovereignty is granted.

The greatest example of this trickery and deception is the entire third-dimensional matrix reality built around and perpetrated on humanity without their knowledge. All the matrix systems, including religion, politics, news/media, government, corporations, labor, law, big pharma, and education, are designed to harvest human energy. Everything in the third-dimensional matrix is an intentionally-distorted illusion that has nothing to do with natural and true reality. This matrix trickery is a giant cult magic show and the greatest illusion in the universe designed to drain every ounce of human energy during one's life on Earth. If you ask, "Who is orchestrating this manipulation of Earth?" It's just a few fourth-dimensional beings with serious egos that set this control structure up 350,000 years ago, and it has been going strong up until now. The good news is that when you become a sovereign master, every contract with these beings is made null and void concerning you!

The next way to grant consent for one's energy to be used by another is by allowing the experience of negative emotions. Some might argue that feeling negative emotions is normal, but we can tell you it is not normal. A primary part of ascension mastery is to keep one's vibration elevated, and a normal state of emotion is to experience peace, joy, and love. When one vibrates low and allows negative emotions, they are not only creating pain and suffering for themselves but also making a statement to the universe that they are allowing and agreeing with this lower state of being. This free-will agreement to vibrate low creates a condition of contractual agreement to bring in even more low energies into one's energetic space. When one reaches and stabilizes a vibration that matches the fifth dimension, one will never experience another low, painful emotion.

Consent can also be granted for one's energy to be taken and used by not caring for oneself or the things in their life lovingly and healthily. This can include indulging in unhealthy addictions and habits. Ingesting unnatural substances, drugs, or alcohol is a direct way of granting consent for the worse kinds of energy manipulation by low-vibrational beings. Living in any debased way without pride, cleanliness, good character, or nobility tells the universe one does not care. Saying I do not care energetically says I agree to whatever contract another proposes, even if it harms me.

The most frequent way contractual consent can be granted to have one's energy taken and used is implied consent. Of course, implied consent is a bit shady to begin with, but in this universe, it's enough to create an enforceable contract between two parties. One's actions, of course, can be used to create implied consent for a contract, but more specifically, by not saying 'no' or by not saying or doing anything means one said 'yes.'

Suppose you are energetically attached to a friend, who is connected to another unhealed person who vibrates very low, and you are unaware of this other person. It is implied and understood that you know what you are doing by being connected to the original friend, so you are saying 'yes'; it's ok to be connected to the other person. In this case, you agreed contractually by implied consent to have your life-force energy used by an unhealed being you are unaware of.

Again, this is where correct awareness is required of what is transpiring around you so you have enough information to act accordingly. Make sure you know who and what your closest connections are connected to!

Surely there couldn't be even more ways to gain this contractual permission to steal the energy from the free-will beings of Earth. But it turns out, yes, there is! How about using fear, force, or threat to create a contract? That's the ultimate way to get someone to agree to just about anything, even something harmful. If a controlling power was clever enough, it might come up with false terror events, false news narratives, false justification for wars, military threats or actions, and all types of false fear scenarios to try and gain control over entire populations for selfish and harmful reasons. If one can threaten and intimidate another with enough fear, they can gain complete access to their energy. The ones intimidated this way will likely consent to just about any contract if they become fearful enough.

The basic fear of survival is one of the strongest intimidation tactics for creating a harmful contract. The commercial debt matrix was created in a compartmentalized and secret way to gain the complete implied consent for an entire planet to be dominated in so many ways. The monetary foundation of the commercial matrix system is based on scarcity, debt, and lack, which creates a constant state of fear of survival. There is never enough, and one must work hard their entire life on Earth for someone else to mainly survive.

Of course, the idea of scarcity on Earth is a complete illusion among the obvious unlimited resources available on this planet.

Whatsmore, the monetary foundation of the commercial matrix system is itself a grand illusion. All Earth money is, in reality, simply fiat or quasi money or promissory notes. Worse, not one ounce of gold or silver backs up all this illusionary commercial value. The entire monetary system is based on debt, not money, and under this harmful system, the one in debt is considered slave property and an indigent criminal. In this debt matrix, you can only pay a debt with a debt. This debt-based money system is much more complex and sinister than one might imagine. As one looks deeper into its inner workings, one will quickly see the greatest crime ever perpetrated against humanity.

In this third-dimensional matrix commercial system, it is assumed by implied consent that every person in this system is not a sentient being but is instead a corporate entity. What's more, all these corporations are claimed to be the owned property of the state. Therefore, it is assumed by implied consent that one agrees to this fictional commercial matrix game because they live in it, interact with it and depend on it. As we said, one says yes to this by not saying no.

All systems of Earth law, crime, and punishment are based solely on commerce, which is a very profitable business. For example, the title or deed to each person on Earth is the birth certificate, a publicly traded commercial instrument. Furthermore, as soon as an Earth human goes to prison, a hidden multi-million-dollar bond is created behind the scenes that begins trading on the stock market. It trades until the bond matures or until the person gets out of prison. Likewise, marriage contracts, social security cards, driver's licenses, and all court documents are commercial instruments with tremendous market value.

Every statement, every notice, and every traffic ticket one receives in the commercial matrix is a financial instrument. It is assumed by implied consent that one is expected to foot the bill since one lives in the commercial matrix and enjoys its services. An example is when one receives a bill in the mail. The bill implies that one owes what is written on it, whether they do or not, and the bill is considered an enforceable contract. As soon as a presentment, bill or notice is made to a person; they are already considered to be in commercial dishonor because they owe a debt. Ignoring a presentment or not replying to it correctly is considered an even worse commercial dishonor. The same goes for notice or note, short for promissory note. In the commercial matrix, the only crime is to owe a debt. This makes every citizen of planet Earth a criminal because there is only debt in the matrix.

In Earth's law and court terminology, this is where the word 'charge' comes in. One is considered responsible for paying any commercial contract presented to them in the matrix. As we said, this is all about energy, so think of the magic words 'currency' and 'circuit' court related to electrical energy. When you received that bill, you were charged with 'The energy to take action or act.'

Did you notice the magic word 'act,' as in acting in a fictional drama or play? Think of the phrase, 'acting judge.'

Also, a 'court' is simply the playground of commercial instruments where contractual presentments are passed back and forth between corporations, like playing ball. Since sentient beings are presumed to 'not exist in the corporate commercial matrix, a living being has no rights there and may not speak in court. They have no rights and cannot speak because they are presumed to be non-living, dead, not real, and not there at all. This is why they must have an attorney, a corporate agent of the king's court, to speak for them. Sentient beings must also 'appear' in court like a ghost would manifest. One can appear there, like a shadow, but in the corporate matrix, it is understood they cannot possibly be there physically and are not even allowed to be there, period. An irrebuttable presumption of guilt is unconstitutional in the United States; however, an arrest means one is considered guilty until proven innocent. The reason for this is, as we said, there are no rights for sentient beings in the commercial matrix. Before one can be officially charged in court, one must agree to a contract that contains clauses that usually cannot be understood. There is an unspoken law that says commercial courts do not have jurisdiction over sentient beings, and if this is understood deeply enough, one finds out this is true. It is not just a phrase one blurts out in court because that may not work out well. Maritime law courts (all courts) only have jurisdiction over corporations, called 'persons. A legal person is a corporation superimposed over a sentient being as their identity, and this corporate identity takes on the form of an upper-case name.

Ultimately, all the contract methods mentioned above are not valid for creating contracts; these methods only create illusory contracts. Contracts that do not have all the terms conveyed or disclosed clearly and thoroughly are considered void from the beginning and are not enforceable. We rest our case.

"Light is information, and darkness is the lack of information."
The Pleiadians

If you had known that some harmful thing was concealed in a contract, you certainly would not have agreed to that contract.

Most Earth humans truly do not know they exist in this fictional commercial matrix control world, and they certainly do not understand the rules governing it. Even more importantly, most never reach the stage where they break free and become independent of it.

Here is the remedy, and here is relief.

"Be sovereign in all your ways."
The Pleiadians

Expanding one's consciousness is the first major step toward freedom and sovereignty. One must be fully aware of what is transpiring around themselves, on many levels, at all times. When one has information, they have light, which becomes the light that shines into the deepest, most hidden levels of darkness. It is said, "When the light shined in the darkness, the darkness could not understand it, so it fled away."

It is first advised that one gains a deep inside knowledge of exactly how this commercial matrix system works. What is discovered will be shocking; however, don't get stuck there after seeing the truth; one must accept what it is and quickly move higher.

Next, gain full knowledge about living a sovereign lifestyle and create a liberating plan.

At the beginning of this chapter, we said all beings are already sovereign; however, this sovereignty can be lost if one gives away their power in an unconscious way. Therefore, if this has occurred, the only way to correct it and become sovereign again is to take back one's power.

The most powerful and fastest way to achieve liberating energetic results in one's life is to begin working with the universe. We tell you, the universe has your back and will send you well on your way toward sovereignty.

Since this universe operates under contracts and laws, a built-in, tangible remedy prevents any being from controlling or manipulating your energy without permission.

The remedy is simply to decree that one does not consent to any energy manipulation, and it must stop by universal law.

If you do not believe this, try it.

The first step to re-establishing sovereignty is to speak the following personal decree aloud several times per day for a few days:

"My personal power is my personal power. My life force is my life force. No one can use my energy without my permission, and I do not give permission. Therefore, I am revoking all contracts in my life, known and unknown, and I shall reinstate new contracts of my choice that will serve my highest good. So it is."

When you speak the decree above, say it out loud, as you mean it, and place great emotion behind the words. When a decree like this is spoken, it invokes unimaginable universal power that will come to your aid, and you will notice in time that things that once bound you in life no longer have any power and must let go. What you say to the universe is the highest binding contract that exists, and these powerful words shall indeed manifest as one's new sovereign reality.

The fifth dimension is the dimension where one first speaks their highest truth. Sometimes this highest truth might be the word "no." Before being ascended in consciousness, one most likely allowed others to use their energy in unhealthy, even harmful ways, simply because one did not say no. Sovereignty is about speaking the truth and then living it. Learn to say 'no' and set safe, energetic boundaries. You have the free will of conscious choice to say yes or no, and this is your way of making contractual agreements work in your favor. This works not only with the universe but also on an everyday level anytime someone presents anything to you, be it a document, a thing, spoken words, or something energetic. To perfect this contracting skill, when something is presented, ask yourself, "How does this feel to me?" You have every right to say no if it doesn't resonate with you. Keep in mind that there is a specific art to saying 'no,' especially in response to commercial contracts, where you will always remain in honor, and it is advised that you study and work on perfecting this art. As we teach in our Ascension Chapter, one must set firm, healthy boundaries around their being and create space when necessary. This is a primary part of self-love and healthy self-respect. As one sets these energetic boundaries, very real universal forces enter to ensure one has relief and remedy and that things unfold quickly in their favor.

The next step towards energetic freedom is to make a written, lawful decree of personal sovereignty and file it correctly into the record. The primary reason for this is that a new contract is placed into force that overrides all previous contracts, which will govern your being accordingly. Make sure you rely on credible and lawful sources when preparing and presenting these sovereignty documents, and only take wise counsel from a master on this subject. If this process is done correctly and lawfully, a new public contract on record will be attached to you that will work quietly behind the scenes in your favor.

Once you have a thorough knowledge of how all of this works, the next time you receive a commercial matrix presentment of any sort, see the presented contract simply as an 'offer to contract,' so make an intelligent and lawful counteroffer. You may be surprised how things work out in the end.

"You are the king or queen of your kingdom."
The Pleiadians

Practice self-reliance and self-sufficiency, and live as best as possible without relying on anyone else. First, you must ensure you can produce and provide everything required for daily survival. This includes water, food, shelter, heat, and oxygen is a given. Beyond this, one must have safety/security, sleep, and health. Beyond that is a myriad of things depending on how elaborate one desires their life to be. The less one interacts with the third-dimensional matrix system and the corporations that make it up, the less power this control system has over them. This includes sharing too much of one's personal life force energy with lower vibrational Earth beings. Living a bit off the grid not only makes space between oneself and low-vibe beings of Earth but also creates energetic space from the harmful commercial matrix system.

Learn to live naturally and devise creative and economical ways to produce what you need. The information about how to do this is readily available if you seek it. Though you are an island to yourself, you will attract many like-minded supporters who respect your lifestyle and will always be there for you.

A positive thing about living a sovereign lifestyle on the land is that when natural disasters or other troubles and trials come to the populated world, one is set up in a safe space and is prepared for what may come. Therefore, it is much more likely that a sovereign living on his own land, providing for their own needs, would survive a major disaster than the masses of Earth beings who dwell in cramped cities that do not live this way.

Practice self-governance and govern yourself accordingly. Take responsibility for your life 100%. The sovereign consciously creates their own reality and knows their personal manifested reality is their sole responsibility. There are no victims, and there is no one to blame. Sovereign beings do not require authority figures, gods, or leaders, and they live as such. A sovereign being does what they desire and does not violate the will of others. Sovereign beings keep their word and fulfill all valid contracts in honor. A sovereign being always operates from the highest state of love and peace. A master of sovereignty knows that sovereignty is no excuse for any harmful crime or action. Therefore, they strive never to do harm. The sovereign knows this is the one true law that fulfills all law systems. If harm is done in some unexpected way, they take full responsibility and make it their prime duty to make things right as fast as they can, to the best of their ability. They know this is the way of the master.

Something magical happens when one becomes sovereign. This is where one grows up. It is time to grow up and take on the ultimate responsibility. It's time to be honorable and begin displaying the highest character levels. These ways of being are primary requirements for universal sovereignty. Start being the highest and most grand version of yourself that you can conceive of and begin to live out of your heart completely. This is what sovereignty is all about, and when you begin to be and live this way, you will become fully enlightened.

Chapter 12: Manifesting

"Consciousness is the cause of all things."
The Pleiadians

What if one could manifest real magic into their life and this world? If there were no limits to what one could be, do and have, what kind of life would you begin to create?

The principle of cause and effect. "Every cause has its effect; every effect has its cause; everything happens according to law; chance is but a name for law not recognized; there are many planes of causation, but nothing escapes the law."
The Kybalion

As an awakened Starseed, you are aligning more and more each day with your true identity. On your great evolutionary journey, you have probably already experienced the grand awareness that you are no less than God, dwelling in a human body. But, of course, when pondering this ultimate identity, one must also conclude that they have potentially unlimited abilities. You are a creator god; your most remarkable ability is creation itself. You can create anything that you desire using conscious energy.

It's important to note that the word 'creator' is not precisely the right word for this teaching, and here's why. Everything in the universe is already created, so a better word to describe your divine power to bring things forth would be 'manifest.' To manifest something means to 'make it appear,' which sounds like magic, yes? Everything was indeed created all at once by God/you at a beginning point. Since then, you have simply been choosing from one or more of your existing universal creations.

The Earth science of quantum physics is derived from advanced Pleiadian sciences. This science explains how every possible configuration of everything in the universe already exists in energetic form in the quantum field as waves of possibility, and these energy waves are converted into physical reality. As we discussed in our Light Chapter, this energetic form, the foundation of all things, is the base informational field of the universe and has been called the Akash, the quantum field, source energy, or simply all that is. This universal, informational field is called 'light' by the Pleiadians.

The Pleiadians are proficient at manifesting and materializing matter, and they do this by converting light into matter. They know that all matter is constructed from light. As a light being, you also have the unlimited ability to mold this light into any material object or reality you desire.

Now let's go super quantum. How does one transform light into matter? Some say it can't be done, and some have said they have done it recently by smashing particles together. We say it has been done since time eternal and is being done infinitely, in every moment. We also say it is all a very natural process built into one's being, and it is quite simple to achieve.

"Without consciousness, there would be no physical world, only probabilities of existence."
The Pleiadians

Matter is instantly created from light when a probability wave function collapses. So a probability wave function is matter's potential existence, and these possible things are the real things in their energetic form.

How is a probability wave function collapsed?

A probability wave function is collapsed into matter when consciousness observes it. Consciousness and matter are inextricably entangled, and matter cannot exist without consciousness. Reality is information or light-based, not matter-based. Consciousness is fundamental in this universe, and matter depends solely on consciousness. Another way to say matter (physical reality) is created from light (information) is to say, "You manifest what you see, or what you look at, exists."

When energy descends or lowers its frequency, it's transformed into matter. The frequency of energy is slowed down when it is interacted with by consciousness. This looking and observing collapses the energy into a dense state of perceived solid matter. This is the secret to all of quantum physics. Matter is not matter; it is energy or waves captured or suspended in a reality frame and projected or manifested holographically as perceived outward physical matter or particles. All manifested reality is only perceived reality. "Seeing, looking, or observing" are broad words regarding manifesting. To observe in quantum physics also means to focus on, give energy to, think about, feel, align with, or resonate with. This observing force is the force of consciousness that collapses the wave function and materializes a thing into the physical world.

In this universe, energy attracts like energy 100% of the time. Therefore, frequencies that resonate at the same level are attracted to each other.

It is important to know that one is always manifesting their perceived reality, whether conscious or unconscious, of the process. This means that one has created everything in their life up to this point using this universal process and whether the manifestation is worthy of one or not is something one may consider. If it isn't, one can always begin creating something entirely new.

Here are the primary techniques for mastering the art of manifesting.
Of course, having a high level of conscious awareness is the first requirement for manifesting. Be very aware that you are doing this already, in an automatic way, in every moment; however, the default state of unconscious manifesting produces many things in life that are not desired. Therefore, the only way to be in control of one's life is to

become a conscious manifester that brings forth what is desired intentionally.

Also, be aware that your manifestations' quality, speed, and power depend solely on your vibrational frequency.

Similarly, know that you cannot receive what you desire if you do not know what you desire.

If you ask several people what they desire most in life, you might be surprised that some have no idea, and they will say, "I never thought about it much."

Sit down in a sacred space and write what you desire the most. Cover all areas of life and include the intricate details of each thing on the list. This list can change if a desire changes, and it is good to revisit and review your list frequently.

Since everything is already created and exists in unlimited versions and variations in energetic form, your divine ability and work are to align your being with what you desire vibrationally, and your desires have no choice but to manifest before you.

A powerful way to achieve this alignment is to fully saturate your being, senses, and emotions with the thing you desire to manifest.

One must also fully experience the desire in the 'now' moment because now is the only time a thing can manifest or exist. Therefore, in your alignment work, feel how good it feels in a full-sensory way to have the thing you desire now. When you achieve this alignment, you will feel as if you already have your desire, and only then will it manifest.

The universe has a unique built-in notification system that lets you know the status of your manifestation. This universal system is called 'synchronicity.' If you are in alignment vibrationally with your manifestation, the universe will flash a special message designed just for you at the right moment. Synchronicity is where an external event mirrors an internal one. Synchronicities may appear as numbers, codes, text, and symbols, but they can also be events, things appearing, or people showing up. Their unique timing, wonderous and obvious content, which only has meaning to you, and the way they are usually connected to one or more other things causes them to be special and greatly defy all odds. It's important to look for them consciously because consciousness is their source. Because of the way all things are entangled in this universe at the energetic level, the synchronicities become more frequent and more profound as the manifestation gets closer to appearing. On your way to manifesting, you will experience these magical synchronicities and know how to decode their message. These divine messages say, "You are right on track, and your wildest dreams are about to come true."

You also have a built-in manifesting messaging system called your 'emotional guidance system.' On your manifesting journey, ask yourself how you feel about a specific manifestation, and your emotions will give you its status. If you feel good about it, it is coming into your life at the speed of light! Conversely, it moves further away if you doubt or fear the manifestation. The good news is that you completely control this system, so make any adjustments to your vibe as needed.

Many first learned about the reality manifestation process years ago from excellent teachers speaking about quantum physics, the great secret, and the law of attraction. This was a big eye-opener on planet Earth, and it certainly set the starseeds of Earth on the right path to conscious manifesting. However, despite the incredible level of conscious awakening this information created, many attempted the practices of the great secret but only sometimes achieved optimal results. Sometimes it worked, but many times it didn't.

Beyond the primary techniques, we listed above, here is a deeper Pleiadian understanding of how manifesting works.
For starters, we call manifesting that doesn't work so well 'third-dimensional manifesting' and

manifesting that always works, with no exception, 'fifth-dimensional manifesting.'

How fifth-dimensional manifesting works.
You have two brains, or two minds, the left brain, and the right brain. These two brains both serve very important purposes, work differently, and usually do not work together. Your left brain is the conscious mind, and your right brain is the subconscious mind. The left brain is the logical brain, the thinking mind, and the subconscious mind is the creative mind. This creative attribute is the first clue about what the subconscious mind is. The conscious mind is third-dimensional, and the subconscious mind is fifth-dimensional. The conscious mind acts like a gatekeeper for the subconscious mind. Programs do not easily get past the conscious mind and into the subconscious mind under normal conditions. Concerning intelligence and computing power, the conscious mind is like a 486 computer, and the subconscious mind is a billion times more

powerful and operates exactly like a quantum computer. This is where the inspiration for developing a quantum computer came from. Though incredibly powerful and multi-dimensional, the subconscious mind learns and executes programs differently from the conscious mind. The subconscious mind functions like a tape player that automatically plays back recorded programs that operate every aspect of daily life. When we say programs, we mean programmed knowledge sets, body function programs, belief systems, ways of thinking, ways of feeling, and ways of being. On top of its daily down-to-Earth functions, the subconscious mind has access to advanced universal data and computes this complex data faster than the speed of light. The subconscious mind is also connected directly to one's higher self. One can only access their higher self when one has access to the subconscious mind.

The subconscious mind runs 97% of your daily life. It has been in control and running the show since you were born on Earth. There is usually little, or no conscious awareness of the subconscious mind's programs or operations as it is beyond the range of conscious perception. This quantum mind controls your very breath and heartbeat at every moment.

So which mind is in charge of manifesting?

The left brain, the conscious mind, is where one conceives and visualizes the dreams and desires about what one wants to manifest. This mind creates ideas, dreams, and plans, writes lists, makes vision boards, does affirmations, thinks positively, gives gratitude, and focuses with all its might on its desire. The problem is that the conscious mind has little to do with the actual manifesting process. On the other hand, the subconscious mind is a quantum mind that operates beyond time and space and is the sole mechanism for collapsing a probability waveform instantly. The subconscious mind creates matter from energy, or matter from light, instantly. The manifestation has a zero-time gap because this quantum mind operates outside of time and space.

Whether the subconscious mind has a program that says I have a red $100,000 tesla, I am a billionaire, or I can fly, that energetic program will manifest as an instant physical reality.

So far, so good; however, a serious issue arises at this point:

Almost every program put into the subconscious minds on Earth since birth is disempowering. Since this mind attracts similar energy to itself, it manifests all kinds of disempowering things into one's life by default. Moreover, it has been doing this since day one. The subconscious has been filled with bad programs for almost every being on third-dimensional Earth. These have been fed in from the low-vibrational matrix and past habits and experiences composed mostly of trauma and drama. As a result, these disempowering programs have been instantly manifesting as one disempowering event after another.

It does no good to attempt to visualize and create a better reality using the normal conscious mind manifestation methods to overturn any bad programs because the subconscious supercomputer mind will rise and overturn any conscious mind manifestation plans every time. The subconscious mind will dominate and always win in every case. This is what it is supposed to do and how it was created.

Then one may ask, "I create my dreams and desires in my conscious mind, so if the conscious mind has little or no effect on the actual manifesting process, and since the subconscious runs the show and is full of disempowering matrix programs, running 97% of my life, how can I get around this?"

First, one must realize they must work directly with the subconscious mind to manifest anything into the physical world. However, achieving this is about as near to impossible as it gets because the subconscious mind is off-limits to your consciousness, with only one exception.

Programs can be directly entered into the subconscious mind during an alpha brainwave state.

What is the alpha brainwave state? An alpha brainwave state is a state of being that resonates from eight to twelve hertz and occurs in a relaxed state after left-brain conscious thinking ceases. In this state, the conscious mind synchronizes with the right higher subconscious mind. Alpha is a state of super learning where access to the higher self is granted via the right brain, which opens up a new realm of unlimited possibilities.

Though only an alpha brainwave state opens a direct door to the subconscious mind, there are several modalities for creating an alpha brainwave state, and these are:

- Hypnosis.
- Deep meditation.
- Hemi-sync tones/programs.
- Repetition/training/practice.
- New energy psychology modalities such as psych-k.

The best time to achieve an alpha brainwave state is bedtime before falling asleep. The fastest way to manifest a new empowering program into the subconscious is using Hemi-sync tones/programs. If one plays a Hemi-sync program in their headset just before sleep, the program bypasses the conscious mind and goes straight into the subconscious mind. The subconscious mind will quickly manifest the information in the program into its material reality every time. Remember the real magic here; it can do this instantly, with no time delay. Think about that for a moment.

This is only the beginning of a supergalactic trip, however. As we said in our Time and Space Chapters, an alpha brainwave state gives one full access to an out-of-body state where one can literally and physically teleport, change physical timelines/realities, or accomplish every other divine and magical thing one can think of. The effects of an alpha brainwave state are well-known and scientifically proven by several prominent groups who have studied and evaluated its power. We encourage you to research these methods to see what you can manifest and achieve in the alpha state. Then, begin to use these modalities and download new programs directly into the subconscious to radically change the character of your life in just a matter of minutes.

One can make this whole subconscious reprogramming process much more powerful and effective by syncing their heart to their brain. While the brain sends the electrical thought signal to the end of the universe, thought alone is not enough for any significant manifestation because there is no mechanism to bring the thought back as a physical form. The heart field is the emotional magnetic force that pulls the manifestation back into the physical realm. The heart is the jet engine in the universal manifestation process and makes the process one thousand times more powerful. The heart's energy is the real power behind the universal law of attraction.

The more understanding one gains of consciousness, energy, quantum physics, and manifesting, and the more one puts these principles into practice, the more wonderful and amazing life will be. When one gains this knowledge, one can then call themselves a master manifester who displays tangible results in the physical realm.

Everything in this book has led to this last step of manifesting matter into the physical world. As we worked our way down in each chapter through the magnificent energies of the universe, isn't it interesting at the end of the day how this unimaginably powerful and magical energy is designed and set up to support you and your physical life on Earth?

Closing

It is by no accident that the knowledge contained in this book has been given to you. We want you to know that there is great purpose in everything, and we wrote this book just for you.

Keep this book close to you to serve as a light for your spiritual and physical journey on Earth.

Read it again later, contemplate even deeper on what is said, take notes and begin doing what you do best, create!

God-speed,
Michael and The Pleiadians

"Now you have become the master!"
The Pleiadians